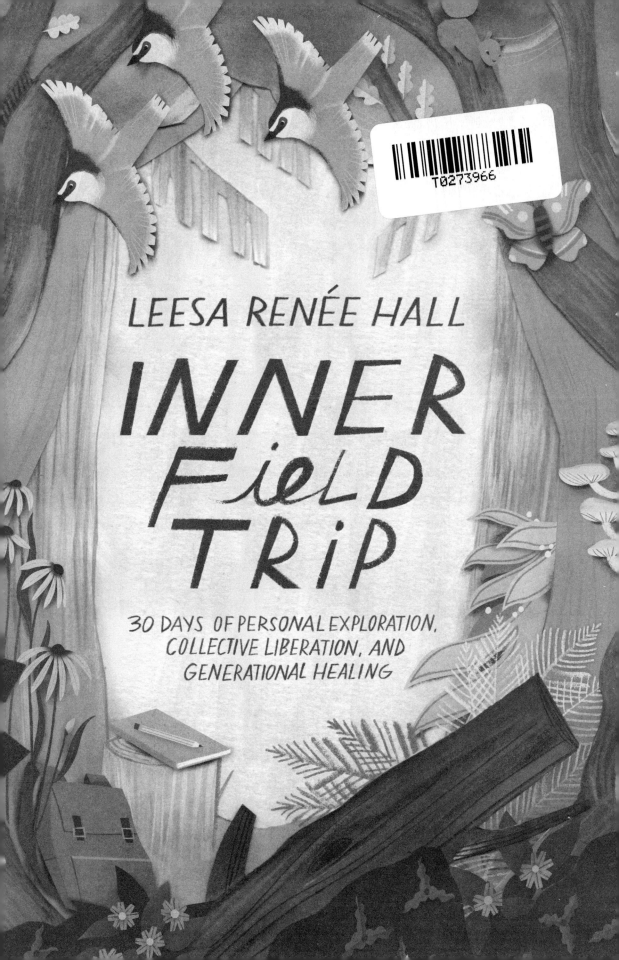

LEESA RENÉE HALL

INNER FiELD TRIP

30 DAYS OF PERSONAL EXPLORATION, COLLECTIVE LIBERATION, AND GENERATIONAL HEALING

*Row House Publishing recognizes that the power of justice-centered storytelling
isn't a phenomenon; it is essential for progress. We believe in equity and
activism, and that books—and the culture around them—have the potential to
transform the universal conversation around what it means to be human.*

*Part of honoring that conversation is protecting the intellectual property of authors.
Reproducing any portion of this book (except for the use of short quotations for review
purposes) without the expressed written permission of the copyright owner(s) is strictly
prohibited. Submit all requests for usage to rights@rowhousepublishing.com.*

*Thank you for being an important part of the conversation
and holding sacred the critical work of our authors.*

Library of Congress Cataloging-in-Publication Data
Available Upon Request

ISBN 978-1-955905-29-9 (TP)
ISBN 978-1-955905-40-4 (eBook)

Printed in the United States
Distributed by Simon & Schuster

First edition
10 9 8 7 6 5 4 3 2 1

Contents

PART 1
Before the Quest

DAY ONE

DAY TWO

DAY THREE

DAY FOUR

DAY FIVE

DAY SIX

DAY SEVEN

PART TWO
During the Quest

PART THREE
After the Quest

Introduction

"I'm aware of my advantages, but I'm tired of the conversation."

Those words were uttered on social media by an influencer who had performed quite a number of actions to dismantle systemic oppression. They read the books. They watched the documentaries. They listened to the podcasts. They had tough conversations. They attended the marches. They put together and shared a list of anti-oppression or anti-bias educators. They created a one-year diversity, equity, and inclusion plan for their business.

But the influencer didn't stop there. They also donated to every crowdsourcing project. They changed their profile image on their socials to a colored square, showing their solidarity. They apologized for their ancestors' oppressive actions. They confronted Uncle Bigot and Grandma Intolerant at the last family gathering. They added their identified pronouns to their email signature and listed land acknowledgments on their website. They posted a long missive on their socials declaring all the ways that they planned to do and be better.

They became aware, jumped into action, and now, after several weeks or months of frantic activity, they're tired. Tired of talking about unmerited advantages that they didn't ask for. Tired of guilt and shame. Tired of feeling hopeless. Tired of being called out for messing up. Tired of being disappointed. Tired of the confusion due to one person saying to do activism one way and another saying something completely different. Tired of the anger and outrage. Tired of doing so much, so often, and for so little. Tired of being tired.

Maybe you're feeling exhausted, too. You became aware of injustice, so you jumped into action. You marched for Black lives. You posted on your socials to Stop Asian Hate. You called out your friend for using ableist words. You argued with your family member about reproductive rights. And then, yet another video is published showing a racist, Islamophobic, homophobic, sexist, xeno-phobic, or ableist act.

Or, maybe it's not the social justice actions that are leaving you fatigued. Maybe it's the way your body feels. Your nervous system, muscles, and heart are in a constant state of high alert. You are sensitive, intuitive, and empa-thetic. You care deeply about other humans. Seeing pain and suffering due to identity-based oppression is just too much. You are not just feeling exhausted; you're feeling overwhelmed.

If you're a person who experiences identity-based oppression yourself, your fatigue is different. While you, too, may be tired of taking action, you're even more exhausted protecting yourself from microaggressions, minimizations, denials, and dismissals that come from those who hold privilege. They align with you when acts of injustice are shared on social media or in the news, but then they disappear when the spotlight turns to something else. You wish *you* could opt out. You desire to navigate public and private spaces without harassment, surveillance, or abuse.

Allies want to be seen as one of the good ones and stand in solidarity with those who face identity-based oppression. People of the global majority who face identity-based oppression are tired of shielding themselves from injus-tice. What connects us is our desire to use our innate strengths in a positive way. We dream of a future without bias or oppression. As idealists and opti-mists, we believe that humans can do better and unlearn the harmful beliefs that we hold. We envision communities where we treat each other kindly and equally, no matter the identities we hold.

This is the future I want and the values I believe in, too. However, systems of oppression do not suddenly or immediately change just because one person—or even one thousand people or, sadly, ten thousand people—watched a doc-umentary, issued an apology, published a one-year plan, or read out a land acknowledgment. Generations of biases, prejudices, and stereotypes do not vanish because you became aware of them and took on either small tasks or even grandiose projects to help. These symbolic actions rarely lead to sys-temic change, and certainly not on the timeline many who are new to activ-ism hope or expect. Like the influencer above, you likely skipped over a very crucial step. This step could've helped you protect your energy and align with justice using a more sustainable approach.

Taking AIM at Your Unconscious Biases

Dismantling systems of oppression is urgent work. People are being abused, harassed, even killed due to their social, ethnic, biological, or behavioral identities (I'll use SEBBIs for short). Some are unable to navigate private and public spaces freely because they are in the "wrong" body.

I can understand the desire to rush into action after becoming aware. Urgency, however, is a trait of the dominant culture (you'll learn more about this on Day 13 of our Inner Field Trip™ itinerary). You have been socialized to believe that you need to take quick action *right now*. Self-reliance is another trait of the dominant culture. You have learned that if you want something to change, you must take personal responsibility to make it happen, and that you and you alone must and can be pivotal in changing the world—and, again, you must do so immediately. This thought process leads to attempts to "rescue" and "save" the oppressed. The dominant culture has taught you that marginalized people are not smart enough to solve their own problems. So, you must swoop in and provide your guidance and protection.

Do you see the problem? Through generations of socialization, you have become competent in the ways that the dominant culture has harmed marginalized people. Yet, you lack competency in the ways you use the dominant culture as a weapon against the very people you are trying to help—or even against yourself. This leads to short-term "overachieving" in a way that puts more focus on you and your efforts than on the agency of marginalized people themselves, or on organizations that are already doing deeply entrenched and longtime work.

Why does this matter? Well, if you're only activated when you're outraged, or if you only go to marches to feel good about yourself or be thought well of by others or because you expect immediate results, then you'll abandon social justice causes once the spotlight turns to someone or something else or that first burst of adrenaline has faded. Systems of oppression took generations to take shape; it'll take more than one march (or donation or petition or statement on your socials) to dismantle them.

Let me be clear—the marches, petitions, and donations matter. However, if you're not also taking AIM at your unconscious biases, then you won't feel a lasting, intrinsic, and sustainable connection to the work. An unconscious bias is a hidden or unknown prejudice or stereotype held by an individual towards a person, place, or thing. You can hold an unconscious bias against a particular fruit, a certain neighborhood, or a group of individuals. A bias differs from a belief. A belief is an opinion or conviction that something is true. In a way, a belief sounds like a bias. They're both based on opinions deemed to be true. But unlike a belief, bias is an opinion rooted in inequality, inequity, and injustice. In other words, a bias results in treating a person, place, or thing unfairly.*

AIM is a three-step process that shows the missing step causing so many well-intentioned people to become so tired and overwhelmed when engaging in activism and advocacy. The three-step process is:

A = AWARENESS

You become cognizant that something is not right. You are a bit shaken by what is revealed. Books, films, and educators can help you make sense of and name what is happening.

I = INTERRUPT

You use tools to self-interrogate and self-inquire as to why what you believe vs. how you behave are in deep conflict. This is a process that either encourages you to keep digging into the unknown, or return to the status quo that the dominant culture offers.

M = MOTION

You design an action plan for which causes, charities, and community groups you will amplify (using your privilege if you hold dominant identities, and finding those who can help you heal and work together if you hold nondominant identities). You are not going to take over or launch your own—certainly not as a first or second step. Instead, you support those already doing the work of moving us towards a world without bias, oppression, or bigotry.

---

* Systemic biases are known or unknown prejudices and stereotypes held by institutions. Institutions include those in finance, law enforcement, education, media, entertainment, politics, aviation, wellness and fitness, and retail, just to name a few.

*   *   *

WHEN JUMPING FROM A TO M, and skipping over the I, the acronym becomes A.M., which is a manifestation of your ego. It's all about what *you* can do, how quickly *you* can do it, and how soon *you* will be recognized for the hard work you're doing. Centering is a trait of the dominant culture, so it's no surprise that even the kindest, nicest person uses rugged individualism (another trait of the dominant culture) to tackle inequalities in the fastest way possible (urgency is yet another trait of the dominant culture).

Instead of rushing from the A to the M, you need to interrupt patterns of domination and control that you learned from the dominant culture. Like Cypher from *The Matrix*, you unplugged from the damaging beliefs that were used to obtain your compliance and obedience. Although you chose to unplug from the system of oppression and the institutions and individuals that are complicit in upholding those ways of thinking, you need to spend time unplugging the culture of domination and exploitation that still lives within you.

Being a decent human being isn't awards-worthy. You won't get a shiny medal for finally becoming aware of racism, sexism, transphobia, ableism, or classicism. Instead, you need to get quiet, slow down, and interrogate the ways that urgency, internalized supremacy, binary thinking, defensiveness, right to comfort, elitism, and perfectionism, among other traits of the dominant culture,* still reside within your mind AND body.

Go on an Inner Field Trip

After sharing the AIM framework, I am often asked, "But, Leesa, how do I explore my unconscious biases? What should I do to unplug? Where do I start?" Interrupting your toxic thoughts and interrogating your hidden beliefs can be hard to do. What makes it harder is that there are not a lot of resources that give you the *how to* on what to do.

I could have authored a book about unconscious biases and how they are formed, citing hundreds of evidence-based approaches. Pursuing a graduate

---

* Some of the traits of the dominant culture are similar to the characteristics of a culture of white supremacy that are outlined in a report authored by Tema Okun and Kenneth Jones entitled "Characteristics of White Supremacy Culture."

degree in counseling psychology means that I could've provided you with the biological, social, cultural, psychological, systemic, and political factors influencing the way we think and behave. I could've regaled you with counseling methodologies from some of the pioneers in psychotherapy going back to the late 19th century to show what inspires us to stay ignorant to and stuck in destructive patterns.

There are many books of this nature on the market, and perhaps you have read quite a few already. So, instead, I decided to write what I am most passionate about and believe is largely missing from the marketplace—a practical, step-by-step *activity book* on how to uncover your hidden biases using guided self-reflective methods. Since 2015, I've provided this guidance through my private online community called Inner Field Trip Basecamp (see basecamp .innerfieldtrip.com for more). I'd write prompts and then patrons (that's what founding members in the online basecamp are called, and I'll be using this term regularly in this book) use journaling and expressive arts to explore their hidden prejudices and invisible stereotypes around privilege and power, productivity and work, ancestry and family, and environment and sustainability. To date, tens of thousands of people* have used the Inner Field Trip methodology (guided prompts + self-reflective arts + journaling) to meet their Inner Oppressor (IO), the part of you that pressures and bullies you into submitting to the dominant culture, and explore the difference between what they believe and how they behave.

The Inner Field Trip isn't theory or what I wish would happen. The process to access your innermost trail and meet your Inner Oppressor is based on real people using a proven method to create lasting change. In that time, I've analyzed thousands of reactions that patrons and workshop attendees have shared as they navigated through the Inner Field Trip. Names and identifying details have been changed to protect their privacy. Some quotes have been summarized based on common themes found across several comments. The stories you'll read in this activity book from individuals who completed the Inner Field Trip through the online basecamp and in workshops are based on real people.**

---

* This number is calculated from my Instagram followers, active and formerly active patrons, shares on an October 2017 viral blog post, and attendees at Inner Field Trip workshops.

** I'm thankful to James W. Pennebaker and Joshua M. Smyth for their continued research on expressive writing and for the language around how quotes are presented in this book.

A Guided Self-Reflective Framework

The Inner Field Trip is grounded in an intersectional liberatory healing frame-work.* That's a very wordy way to say that the Inner Field Trip will help awaken you to your unconscious biases in an easeful, gentle, and compassionate way. If you are human, you have unconscious biases. There's no need to deny or be ashamed of them. The problem is trying to identify what type of biases you hold, especially if they're invisible to you. If something is unknown, you can't possibly speak about it. One of the frustrations that can arise when you're sitting in an unconscious bias workshop is that if you don't know the biases are there, how can you talk about them? As a result, unconscious biases become confusing and disorienting.

The Inner Field Trip relies on three tools to help you meet your Inner Oppressor and explore your unconscious biases: guided prompts + self-reflective arts + self-reflective journaling. The image on the following page shows the Inner Field Trip process, along with the outcomes. Using nonverbal and verbal methods to address behaviors and beliefs activates the neurons that connect the hemispheres of the brain so they work together.** Art acti-vates memories; journaling activates the narrative. Together, the intramodal-ity experience brings balance to the mind and body.

If care is not taken when exploring your unconscious biases and meeting your Inner Oppressor, you can self-oppress. When that happens, you'll aban-don the work altogether. The Inner Field Trip was created through the lens of liberation psychology. Liberation psychology, an approach developed in the 1970s by Latin American and Philippine psychologists, is an interdisciplinary approach that "honor[s] multiple ways of knowing and integrating Indigenous, decolonial, postcolonial, anti-racist, ethnic, and transnational approaches into psychology."*** While the Inner Field Trip isn't therapy, it's designed to help you uncover the conflict between what you believe and how you behave using a liberation-informed and culturally responsive approach.

---

* I'm thankful to Kimberlé Crenshaw who coined the phrase "intersectionality" to help us understand the complexity of identity-based oppression.

** Perryman, Kristi, Paul Blisard, and Rochelle Moss. "Using Creative Arts in Trauma Therapy: The Neuroscience of Healing," *Journal of Mental Health Counseling* 41, no. 1 (January 2019): 80–94.

*** Comas-Diaz, Lillian, and Edil Torres Rivera. "Liberation Psychology: Theory, Method, Practice, and Social Justice." *American Psychological Association* (2020): 6.

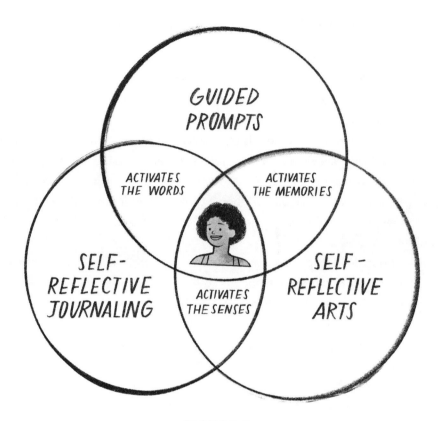

FIGURE 1.

Visual of the Guided Self-Reflective Framework and Outcomes

The guided prompts focus on a specific theme so that your Inner Oppressor knows what to explore. Otherwise, it'll fall silent or take you down an endless rabbit hole. If you look at Days 8–25, you'll notice that each day focuses on a trait of the dominant culture. The guided prompts also let you know that you're not alone. They show you the way, so you don't have to guess, wonder (and wander), or waste time.

Once you and your Inner Oppressor are clear on the theme you're focusing on, you'll then do 15 minutes of self-reflective arts. Art helps to connect you with your body and activates the senses. For example, if you're using clay, it activates your sense of touch. If you're using paints, they activate the movement of the hands. If you're using sound, it activates hearing. When the body is invited into the process, memories come to the surface. You do not need to be an artist to do self-reflective arts; you simply need to be curious. What arises during this brief art modality may not make sense, yet.

Not only are your senses activated when doing self-reflective art, but so, too, are your memories. Art captures the language of the unconscious through symbols, images, and colors.* When you paint with a certain color, draw a particular shape, or illustrate using a distinct pattern, an event or experience can emerge. The memories that speak through art aren't just personal; they can be ancestral as well. In other words, self-reflective art can help you recall narratives from your ancestors. This doesn't mean you'll see or hear your ancestors. When you access ancestral memories, you meet the wise part of yourself (you'll learn more on Day 28). The memories at this stage are often fragmented, and that's when you move to the next step.

Following the 15 minutes of self-reflective arts, you'll do 15 minutes of self-reflective journaling. Also known as expressive writing, therapeutic journaling, or writing to heal, in self-reflective journaling you use pen and paper or keyboard and screen to write in an uncensored, unfiltered, and unedited way until the timer goes off. During this time, you capture the ramblings of your Inner Oppressor. The words that will tumble out onto your page will attach meaning to the stickiness of the pastels on your fingers, the color blue that you used in the doodle, or the swirly shapes you drew in the book. Journaling helps to put words to the unexplainable sensations that were revealed through the self-reflective arts process.

When the timer goes off, you'll either have a clearer understanding of your unconscious biases or more questions that need to be explored. No matter the outcome, this is your invitation to continue the Inner Field Trip.

---

* Sigmund Freud, the founder of psychoanalysis, was the first person documented who identified the existence of the unconscious. He theorized that it contains repressed urges and fantasies. Carl Jung, the founder of analytic psychology, felt that the unconscious did not repress, but expressed messages through symbols, images, and mythologies. Jung's theory of the *active imagination* is a strong influencer of expressive and art therapies.

How to Use This Workbook

This workbook is separated into three sections. You'll spend a few days in Part 1 getting ready. You'll learn what supplies and tools you'll need to start the quest. Part 2 contains Guided Self-Reflective Activities. Each day has a specific dominant culture trait to address, along with the guided prompts and self-reflective art and journaling needed to meet your Inner Oppressor. Part 3 contains tips on how to protect the work you did so you build a sustainable approach to activism and advocacy.

You can skim through the entire book to get an idea of what will be required. However, I do recommend that you not rush through this workbook. Start on Day 1 and give yourself a full twenty-four hours to allow that day's activities to take root.

Because I've taken thousands of people through the Inner Field Trip process, I know what may cause you to stumble (figuratively) along the way. There are a few chapters where I name the challenge that you'll experience and offer some tips on how to move through it. Hence why it's so critical that you go through each day slowly and methodically.

While you go on an Inner Field Trip, you can continue to volunteer, donate, support, and align with the causes and charities fighting for justice. If you want to post about your 30-Day Inner Field Trip quest to your socials, use the hashtag #innerfieldtrip so other Brave Trekkers (that's the name of those, like you, going on this inner journey) can follow along. You'll need community during this quest (you'll learn more about different options on Day 6). Although you're doing the Inner Field Trip by yourself, you are not by yourself.

Now, let's get ready for the quest.

1

Before the Quest

Preparing for Departure

One time while hiking, the heel of my boot broke off. I was two hours into my hike and it was going to take me just as long to get back to the trailhead where I parked my vehicle. I dug into my backpack, found some duct tape, and was able to quickly repair my boot so I could complete the hike.

The best time to plan for a hike is before leaving the house. Not only do hikers plan their route, but they also put items and supplies in their backpack to plan for any and every emergency.

This is the same level of preparation you'll need for the Inner Field Trip. The first seven days are focused on planning when and where you'll engage in the Guided Self-Reflective Activities, what supplies you'll need, and who needs to know what you're doing. In essence, you'll "pack" some supplies into your "backpack" so you're prepared for anything that happens while you're on the quest.

Do not skip over this section and jump right into Part 2. Part of unlearning your need to go fast and do things urgently is to slow down.

Are you ready? Turn the page and start with Day 1.

Take Inventory of Your Identities

As shared in the introduction, the dominant culture dictates which social, ethnic, biological, and behavioral identities (or SEBBIs for short) it deems desirable, favorable, and acceptable.

What are those traits? They are listed below.*

- ✂ **Social traits**—Upper class or wealthy, speak the country's official language with no foreign accent, citizen, property owner, university or college educated, cisgender, Christian, heterosexual, nuclear family, urban or suburban dweller, monogamous, good credit, car owner.

- ✂ **Ethnic traits**—People of the global minority, citizens of a country in the northern hemisphere, non-Indigenous (in settler countries).

- ✂ **Biological traits**—Male, light shade of skin, thin or slim build (for people who identify as women), muscular (for people who identify as men), able body, neurotypical, youthful to middle aged, tall, mentally and physically healthy (disease-free/addiction-free), smooth and light-colored hair (but not gray), few to no freckles, perfect or normal eyesight, narrow nose, right-handed, thin lips.

- ✂ **Behavioral traits**—Outgoing, individualistic, energetic, positive vibes, either/or mindset, present focused, perfectionism, tech

---

* Adapted from Sylvia Duckworth's *Wheel of Power*, Tema Okun and Kenneth Jones's *Characteristics of White Supremacy Culture*, the Canadian Council of Refugees' *Power Wheel*, Manivong J. Ratts's *Dimensions of Identity Model*, and Pamela A. Hays's ADDRESSING framework.

savvy, consumerist, self-reliant, objective/neutral, evidence-based, hustling and grinding, being busy, uniformity, exceptionalism.

A side note: In some countries, the dominant culture prizes different traits. For example, under social traits, Islam may be the preferred religion over Christianity; settled citizens may be preferred in nonsettler countries over migrants; curvy women may be more preferred than thin women; collectivism may be valued over individualism; and a quiet, reserved nature may be favored over a boisterous, expressive one. You may need to make a few adjustments regarding the SEBBIs based on what's true in your country or nation.

If you were born and/or raised in one country but your parents were born and raised in another, this may make identifying dominant SEBBIs difficult. Immigrant parents typically practice the culture they know inside the home even though they are living in a new country with a different culture. As a result, you may have experienced bicultural stress, the pressure to adapt to more than one culture. In this case, I'd recommend that you use the dominant culture that you've had to navigate outside of your home to complete this exercise.

Another factor to take note of is that dominant cultures preferring traits associated with masculinity, such as competition, boisterousness, and independence, may not be desired traits in people who identify as women. If you are a person identifying as a woman, especially one who does not have skin color privilege, you may be called ambitious, pushy, or bossy for possessing the same traits valued in those who identify as men. This can be frustrating and represents another reason why we need to change dominant cultures.

Now, go back over the SEBBIs and circle the traits that are true for you. Slow down. Process each word in a contemplative way. Operate like a vintage browser on dial-up that can't handle the high-resolution images on a webpage. The more SEBBIs you circle, the higher the chance the dominant culture will classify you as a person from a Historically Desired Group (or HDG for short). The dominant culture will allow you to navigate public and private spaces without harassment, surveillance, or questioning. If you do something bad, you are assumed to be innocent even if you are very guilty. Your wrongdoings do not reflect HDG because it is assumed that you acted alone. You can remain oblivious, uninformed, and unconcerned about social injustice and identity-based oppression.

If you did not circle many SEBBIs, the dominant culture would classify you as a person from a Historically Undesired Group (or HUG for short). You cannot navigate public or private spaces freely. As a person from a HUG, you are constantly watched, surveilled, and questioned. Even when this constant surveillance is not intended as menacing, such as someone being curious about your hairstyle, unwanted attention and inquiries constantly interrupt your peace and tranquility. If you do something that is either illegal or against prevailing social norms, it is seen as a reflection of all people within HUG. You are not entitled to your individuality.

What would be excused as "having a bad day" for a person from an HDG is seen as a threat to society if you're a person from a HUG. You must be hyperaware of how you use your emotions because any show of intense emotions can be weaponized against you. If you're passionate about a topic, you're called angry. If you're laughing loudly, you're told to be quiet. If you're quiet, you're looked upon suspiciously. People from an HDG will say that they don't feel safe if you, a person from a HUG, express any emotion. This double standard does not feel fair at all. That's because it is not fair, and yet even many people who agree that it is unfair continue to perpetuate this system of inequity through their unconscious biases.

If you're a person from an HDG who operates with compassion and empathy, you're probably feeling guilty right now and to blame for the fact that you reap advantages while others are unfairly oppressed. You probably feel as though your unconscious biases must be your fault. They are not. Our ancestors created this system; however, it's up to us to change it. For example, let's just say that you inherited a home from your grandparents with a 1930s chic interior complete with metallic wallpaper, decorative iron railings, and a boxy sofa set in vintage beige. Although you didn't have a say in which neighborhood your grandparents bought their home, you can do a complete makeover. You can take the best of what your ancestors gave you and change the areas that need improvement.

If you are feeling like the apostle Paul when he said, "I do not understand what I do. For what I want to do I do not do, but what I hate I do. . . . For I have the desire to do what is good, but I cannot carry it out. For I do not do the good I want to do, but the evil I do not want to do—this I keep on doing,"* there

---

* Romans 7:15, 18–19 (NIV).

is nothing to be ashamed of. You don't have to cower in fear and run from your identities. In fact, if you start wallowing in your guilt and shame around the advantages you hold, this is another form of centering yourself. This will not help change societal circumstances or make life any better for HUGs. Even admitting that you're from a long line of oppressors is a way to move the spotlight from HUGs, if your focus remains there for too long. Centering is yet another way that the dominant culture has conditioned you to ignore the plight of HUGs.

If you are a person from a HUG, as I am, a woman of African descent, I feel your pain. It's not fair that a system exists that penalizes you based on aspects of yourself that you cannot change. If a culture obtains freedom for some by shackling others, then it's a culture that needs to be put to rest once and for all.

But you cannot do it alone. We need to do collective work. As a person from a HUG, you need to be reminded that there is so much good within you. The dominant culture has socialized you to believe that you are inferior and insignificant. However, it is not your fault that the ancestors of HDGs created a system that puts you at a disadvantage. This book is not only intended for those in the HDG demographic but also for you, a person of HUGs, so that you can begin to deprogram the unconscious biases that hold you back.

Your Actions

Step 1—Identify your mood before starting. Go to page 239 and use the Mood Tracker to capture how you're feeling. This will be an action you'll do each day of the Inner Field Trip. Please start the habit now.

Step 2—SEBBIs Cloud (15 minutes).

Supplies needed: Pen, marker or crayon, timer
What to do:
✂ Set your timer to count down from 15 minutes.
✂ Make a word cloud on the blank page containing all the SEBBIs you circled.

Use the space below to draw your SEBBIs Cloud.

Step 3—Journal (15 minutes). *This is your first journaling assignment. Please do not respond to the journaling prompts as if you're filling in a survey. In fact, you are not supposed to respond to all three sets of questions. For instructions on how to navigate through the prompts using the GPS method, read Appendix A before you journal.*

Supplies needed: Sketchbook or journal, pen/pencil OR keyboard and screen, timer.

What to do:
- ✂ Navigate the prompts using GPS (see page 237).
- ✂ Set your timer to count down from 15 minutes.
- ✂ Capture the ramblings of your Inner Oppressor in your journal or sketchbook using the following prompts as a guide:

Prompt #1: What compromises does your Inner Oppressor cause you to make so you present your SEBBIs as more desired? How do you use the favored SEBBIs to hide your marginalized ones?

Prompt #2: Choose your most obscure privilege— the one that isn't obvious or the one you don't think much of. In what ways is this identity a privilege? What words would you use to define this specific privilege? How does your Inner Oppressor use this privilege to suppress others?

Prompt #3: How will you use your desired SEBBIs more responsibly? How will you use your SEBBIs to elevate and not erase people from a HUG?

Step 4—Track your mood after completing the Guided Self-Reflective Activities. Go to page 239 and use the Mood Tracker to capture how you're feeling now that you're done.

Congratulations!

You have completed today's actions. Please resist the urge to move quickly to the next day's actions. If you have capacity, you can also file your Summary Report at https://summary.innerfieldtrip.com (optional). Otherwise, go to page 243 and color in the day that you completed on the Journey Tracker page, put the Inner Field Trip aside, get on with your day, then resume tomorrow.

Decide Who You Are Becoming

When I hike, I do so for personal reasons. I love being on the trail, listening to the animals, and being under the canopy of trees. My soul is refreshed after spending hours hiking. No matter the weather or the season, I'll hit the trails to satisfy an inner desire.

Why do you want to do the Inner Field Trip? Is it to meet an external goal, such as approval from your friends, peers, or coworkers? Or is it to meet an inner desire and satisfy a personal goal? If you do the Inner Field Trip to satisfy an external demand or calm an intense emotion, you'll abandon the quest once you've checked the item off your "being a good ally" checklist or after the vivid emotion has died off.

If you want to finish the Inner Field Trip and make it a part of your daily routine, you'll need to identify a deeper and more personal reason why you want to go on this journey, independent of external demands or intense emotions. In other words, you need to focus more on who you are becoming and less on what you want to accomplish.

According to research shared in James Clear's *Atomic Habits*, when you're trying to create better habits, saying "I want to run a marathon" is an outcome-based goal that many fail to achieve. Even though the person commits to jogging every day right before lunch and may be successful in doing so for a few days, the first time they miss a day, panic sets in and they stop trying to achieve their goal. Clear presents a more sustained method for changing habits and behavior. Instead of forming habits around an outcome, you should instead form habits around an identity, then do small actions each day to prove that that identity is true.

For the Inner Field Trip, instead of saying you want to finish this book or meet a requirement for the Human Resources department, identify who you are already becoming, then prove it to yourself by completing one chapter per day. This will not only help you complete the quest, but it will prevent your Inner Oppressor from treating this as one more achievement to earn or competition to win.

Becoming a Better Ancestor

Often, the idea of identifying who you are already becoming isn't broached within anti-racist or anti-oppressive training. If it is asked, attendees respond with, "I want to be a better ally," which is nebulous and vague. Choosing to be a more aware parent or a more sensitive coworker are great goals, but they keep you focused on the present. In order to truly get the most of the Inner Field Trip experience, you have to adopt a past-present-future mindset. This can be done by grounding yourself in a new identity of becoming a better ancestor.

Why become a better ancestor?

1. To get away from focusing on current trends. A term that is dominant today becomes outdated tomorrow. Ancestors never go out of style because it is something we'll always have and something we'll eventually become. By thinking of yourself as an ancestor, you become more than "trendy" in your thinking and instead become part of the larger system of change extending into the future.

2. To remind yourself that this is generational work. The Iroquois Nation teaches that when making decisions, consider their impact on those who came seven generations before and seven generations after you (also known as 7th Generation thinking). It took generations for your unconscious biases to take shape; it will take more than one Inner Field Trip for them to unravel. This is not something you can rush through. Becoming a better ancestor reminds you to adopt 7th Generation thinking.

FIRE Up Your Legacy

Using the acronym FIRE, here are the four types of ancestors that exist. When you understand that you can become one of these four ancestors, you'll spend the rest of your life lighting a FIRE under your legacy. The four types of ancestors are:

F = FAMILIAL ANCESTOR

Familial ancestors pass on their DNA and cellular memories. As a familial ancestor, you may have biological children of your own or are related to a sibling or cousin who gave birth.

As a familial ancestor, not only do you pass on DNA and cellular memories, but you would pass on stories of your ancestors, as well as the customs and rituals associated with your ancestors' culture. The dominant culture has promised protection, profits, and power in exchange for abandoning one's culture. Skin color, however, is not a culture. As a familial ancestor, you can take responsibility for reviving the traditions of your ancestors and passing them on to your descendants.

A note if you're adopted, estranged from your family, or are a child-free adult:

Some who hear me say that you should become a better ancestor are challenged because they may not know their biological family due to adoption or forced separation. Others may be child-free involuntarily or by choice. The dominant culture has a rigid view of what families should look like, and anyone whose family structure is different is made to feel bad. I remember one workshop attendee, her face wet with tears, shared the following after I explained the three other types of ancestors, in addition to the familial one:

> I don't have children and most likely will not have any. As a single, childless person, I felt so disconnected from all this talk about becoming a better ancestor. I didn't realize that I could pass on other things to the next generation besides my DNA. On the one hand, I'm upset that I've lived so long feeling as if I was unworthy because I don't have children. After seeing the four types of ancestors, I feel like I have purpose. I'm crying due to joy. I can pass on other things to my nieces, nephews, and the other children who are entrusted into my care.

Curious to know what else you can pass onto the next generation besides DNA? Here are the three other ancestors that you can become to FIRE up your legacy.

I = IDEOLOGICAL ANCESTOR

As an ideological ancestor, you'll pass on ideas, inventions, and innovations. Nikola Tesla, Octavia Butler, Harry Jerome, Rosa Parks, Amelia Earhart, Betty White, Toni Morrison, William Lyon Mackenzie King, Terry Fox, James Baldwin, Wayne Gretzky, Joseph Campbell, Martin Luther King Jr., Che Guevara, Bruce Lee, Michael Jackson, Marcus Garvey, and Greta Garbo are examples of individuals who do or do not have children and have shared a body of knowledge with future generations.

You do not need to author a bestselling book, produce an Oscar-winning film, or be adored by millions to become an ideological ancestor. You can create something in your spare time and leave instructions for your estate on what to do with the creation upon your passing. A patron shared that her great-grandmother passed on a book of herbal recipes, which has been given to the eldest daughter in the family. Now that the recipe book was in her possession, she had no clue what to do with it. After learning about becoming an ideological ancestor, she decided to turn her great-grandmother's handwritten recipe book into a print format so she can pass it on to her niece when she gets older. Her grandmother's herbal recipe book has also ignited a desire for this patron to study herbs, giving her a renewed sense of purpose.

R = RELATIONAL ANCESTOR

Do you collect points when you shop at a certain store? Do you get exclusive deals because you're a member of a club? There are advantages to being a member of a group. This is what relational ancestors do. They pass on affinity-based advantages to current and future generations. Membership does, indeed, have its benefits, and you can gain opportunities, even assets, depending on your group affiliation. Relational ancestors are different from familial ancestors because the former is not predicated on DNA.

Examples of groups that pass on affinity-based advantages are sororities, fraternities, alumni associations, trade unions, religions, country or sports clubs, professional associations such as Toastmasters or Business Networking

International (BNI), licensing and regulatory boards, and social change movements, just to name a few. You can obtain membership in these groups and pass on the history, stories, and culture of the group as a relational ancestor.

Some affinity-based groups form for the expressed purpose of dehumanizing and abusing people from a HUG. If your affinity-based advantages are based on the subjugation of others, then you have an obligation to inspire change, or simply let your membership in that group lapse.

E = ENVIRONMENTAL ANCESTOR

An environmental ancestor shares lessons from trees, animals, insects, celestial bodies, rivers, oceans, plants, and seeds, collectively called nature. Nature holds memories that can be applied to how we can adapt to change. Those who have been endowed with the gift to interpret nature's rhythm are the ones who can pass on that knowledge to current and future generations. These environmental ancestors are not just teachers; they are also stewards of nature's memories.

Focus on an aspect of nature that fuels your passion. For me, it is trees. Whenever I need answers, I go hiking and observe trees in their natural environment. If you're inspired by the cycle of the moon, study it deeply, then share its lessons. If it's the way bees live, study their habits, then share what you observe. In her book *Emergent Strategy*, adrienne maree brown points out that the ocean has lessons to teach:

> Have you observed the ocean? The waves are not the same over and over—each one is unique and responsive. The goal is not to repeat each other's motion, but to respond in whatever way feels right to your body. The waves we create are both continuous and a one-time occurrence. We must notice what it takes to respond well. How it feels to be in a body, in a while—separate, aligned, cohesive. Critically connected.*

A word of caution—if you are not indigenous to the lands you live on, I recommend that you yield to those with millennia of knowledge as the primary teachers about the lands and all within it. Colonialism and the Age of Invasion

---

* brown, adrienne maree. *Emergent Strategy: Shaping Change, Changing Worlds*. Chico: AK Press (2017): 16.

inspired explorers, colonists, and early settlers to extract as much from the land as possible. Wars were fought, blood was shed, and people, plants, and animals were forcibly relocated. What settlers and their descendants have been taught is that the land is to be occupied, used, controlled, parceled off, and sold.

If you want to become an environmental ancestor, use your settler advantage to elevate the teachings of those who are indigenous to the lands you live on. To elevate those with deep ancestral knowledge, you often still need to have studied deeply the subjects about which you are passionate. You are just not doing it for your own gain, but rather to amplify the importance of the aspect of nature about which you care about so deeply.

Be wary of using your knowledge for self-elevation and, especially, for financial gain. Even if you have a passion for herbs, seeds, or other parts of nature, for example, you will never be able to learn everything you need to know about these lands because your arrival is too recent. Monetizing your knowledge by hanging a shingle in which you practice ancient, Indigenous healing arts, for example, not only puts you in direct competition with Indigenous people who hold generations of ancestral knowledge, but is also a form of appropriation (you'll explore this on Day 19). Be mindful of how you use your advantages if you want to become an environmental ancestor.

Which Ancestor Will You Become?

The four types of ancestors show that whether you have biological children or not, you can participate fully in leaving a legacy for future generations. You can become one, two, or all ancestors. Whichever you choose, focus on that as your inner desire so you can complete (and repeat) the Inner Field Trip quest.

Your Actions

Step 1—Identify your mood before starting. Go to page 239 and use the Mood Tracker to capture how you're feeling.

Step 2—Fill in the blanks. To FIRE up my legacy, I choose to focus on becoming these types of ancestors:

_____

_____

_____

_____

Step 3—Track your mood after completing the Guided Self-Reflective Activities. Go to page 239 and use the Mood Tracker to capture how you're feeling now that you're done.

Congratulations!

You have completed today's actions. Please resist the urge to move quickly to the next day's actions. If you have capacity, you can also file your Summary Report at https://summary.innerfieldtrip.com (optional). Otherwise, go to page 243 and color in the day that you completed on the Journey Tracker page, put the Inner Field Trip aside, get on with your day, then resume tomorrow.

Schedule a Can't-Miss Meeting with Your Inner Oppressor

No matter how short or long the hike, I put plans in place to ensure that it will be safe and fun. I identify the trail. I schedule the day and time. I pack the right materials and tools in my backpack. I also make sure I have enough food, snacks, and water. Plus, I let my family know where I'm going and when I plan to be back.

This is the same type of planning you'll need to do before going on an Inner Field Trip. While you won't pack a backpack filled with items, you will need to plan when and where you'll do the Guided Self-Reflective Activities. I know you're excited to get into the arts and journaling activities; however, if you rush the process (a trait of the dominant culture), you'll burn out quickly.

Your Inner Field Trip itinerary includes:

- Where and when you plan to do the Guided Self-Reflective Activities (you'll decide this on Day 4)

- What materials you'll need to participate in each Guided Self-Reflective Activity (you'll do this on Day 5)

- How you'll soothe yourself when the Inner Field Trip makes you feel irritated, frustrated, guilty, or sad (Day 6)

- Plus, a strategy on what to do if you miss a day or more (Day 7)

On this day, Day 3, you'll decide on when to do the Inner Field Trip.

When to Do the Inner Field Trip

One way to successfully complete the Inner Field Trip is to schedule a can't-miss meeting with your Inner Oppressor. You'll need to book at least an hour in your calendar each day. The time of the day you choose depends on your mood, work responsibilities, and home-life dynamics.

When I first started taking patrons and workshop attendees on their Inner Field Trips, I insisted that they do it first thing in the morning. I had woken before 5:00 a.m. for 365 consecutive days to go on my Inner Field Trip. *It worked for me*, I thought, *so it'll certainly work for others*.

Rigidity is a trait of the dominant culture, and my inflexibility around what part of the day to participate in the Inner Field Trip meant that some patrons chose not to participate at all. One patron said he'd "sit this one out" because he had young children at home whose wake-up times were unpredictable. Another patron engaged in shift work. "One week, I'll do the evening shift and get home at midnight. There's no way I could wake at 5:00 a.m. to do the Inner Field Trip," they said. Other patrons bitterly complained that they're not a "morning person" and found that waking early was like getting a hair plucked from inside their nose.

I eventually softened my stance once I realized that consistency matters more. I recommend that you choose a time of day that you can commit to daily and where interruptions will be at a minimum. One patron decided to engage in the Guided Self-Reflective Activities just before she picked up her child from school. She arrives half an hour before school lets out for the day, then does the art and journaling until the school bell rings. She found that this was the only time of the day where she could engage in the Inner Field Trip uninterrupted.

Although you'll do the Guided Self-Reflective Activities in 30 minutes (15 minutes of expressive arts + 15 minutes of journaling), schedule an hour to account for the emotions that'll pop up. It's important that you give yourself space for recovery after going through each day of the Inner Field Trip so your body and brain can process what your Inner Oppressor has revealed.

Your Actions

Step 1—Identify your mood before starting. Go to page 239 and use the Mood Tracker to capture how you're feeling.

Step 2—Book a time in your calendar. Schedule a one-hour, recurring, and can't-miss meeting with yourself in your calendar during the portion of the day when you have the least chance of being interrupted. This time would need to be scheduled daily for the remaining 27 days in the Inner Field Trip (not including today, yesterday, or the day before).

Step 3—Fill in the blanks. I booked _____ [time] every _____ [day of the week] as a can't-miss meeting with my Inner Oppressor.

Step 4—Track your mood after completing the Guided Self-Reflective Activities. Go to page 239 and use the Mood Tracker to capture how you're feeling now that you're done.

Congratulations!

You have completed today's actions. Please resist the urge to move quickly to the next day's actions. If you have capacity, you can also file your Summary Report at https://summary.innerfieldtrip.com (optional). Otherwise, go to page 243 and color in the day that you completed on the Journey Tracker page, put the Inner Field Trip aside, get on with your day, then resume tomorrow at the time you booked to meet with your Inner Oppressor.

Create Your Cozy Grotto

Identifying a dedicated spot from which you'll do the Guided Self-Reflective Activities will help you in staying consistent. Will you choose a spot in your bedroom? The kitchen table? Will it be on your apartment balcony or your backyard deck? Inside your car? Where you choose to do your Inner Field Trip is just as important as when. Planning that spot and treating it as a cozy and soft place to land will ensure that you're ready to meet your Inner Oppressor.

A grotto is a spot made to look like a cave, and you can choose to do the Guided Self-Reflective Activities outdoors or indoors at a desk or table. Patrons have taken photos of their cozy grottos and they're located in a variety of places around the home or office. Your cozy grotto does not need to be fancy; it just needs to be comfortable.

When creating your cozy grotto, focus on identifying a spot where you can go each day unhindered. This isn't the time to reorganize your space or get that home remodeling project done. That's not the purpose of your grotto. It needs to be a dedicated spot that tells you that it's time to access your inner-most trail. Remember, it's the consistency that matters when going on an Inner Field Trip.

Other tips in creating your cozy grotto:

- **Add comfort items.** A soft blanket, plush pillow, diffuser, candles, or plants are just some items you can add to your grotto.

- **Ensure that you can access the spot regularly.** If you choose a coffee shop, make sure it's open when you have scheduled the

meeting with your Inner Oppressor. If it's a spot inside the home, make sure family members aren't using that spot for online classes, work meetings, or other activities.

✂ **Weather conditions can be an issue—even indoors.** Choosing a spot outside may satisfy your need to be close to nature; however, your access to that spot may be affected by rain, snow, or fog. Weather can affect a spot indoors as well. If you choose to meet your Inner Oppressor at the kitchen table at 1:00 p.m. and the sun shines so brightly through the window that it makes the space hot, you'll probably need to find another spot.

These small details make a big difference. Make sure you can access your cozy grotto consistently without any obstacles. Sit in the spot during the time of day you plan to meet your Inner Oppressor to ensure that it's not too hot or cold. Choose a spot for your cozy grotto that will nurture, and not hinder, your Inner Field Trip quest.

Your Actions

Step 1—Identify your mood before starting. Go to page 239 and use the Mood Tracker to capture how you're feeling.

Step 2—Explore the space. Navigate your home with the intention of identifying a spot that you'll claim as your cozy grotto. If you plan to do the Guided Self-Reflective Activities outside of your home, go to the spot and make sure it can meet your needs.

Step 3—Fill in the blanks. _____ (location) is where I plan to meet my Inner Oppressor during the time I identified in the previous day's activity.

Step 4—Track your mood after completing the Guided Self-Reflective Activities. Go to page 239 and use the Mood Tracker to capture how you're feeling now that you're done.

Congratulations!

You have completed today's actions. Please resist the urge to move quickly to the next day's actions. If you have capacity, you can also file your Summary Report at https://summary.innerfieldtrip.com (optional). Otherwise, go to page 243 and color in the day that you completed on the Journey Tracker page, put the Inner Field Trip aside, get on with your day, then resume tomorrow at the time you booked to meet with your Inner Oppressor.

Gather the Tools and Materials

O ur biases are messy. We, as human beings, are messy. Because of this, the modality used to explore unconscious biases needs to be messy as well. This is why the Guided Self-Reflective Activities that are part of the Inner Field Trip combine 15 minutes of arts with 15 minutes of journaling. Journaling combined with arts helps your Inner Oppressor become aware of the memories, sensations, and emotions that are locked away inside.

You'll need to assemble the tools to use for Day 8–25 of the Inner Field Trip quest. Below are best practices you can use to prepare for "departure."

Art Tools

For those who join me in a workshop room or online in the Inner Field Trip Basecamp, we use paints, clay, pastels, crayons, canvas paper, sketchbooks, glue, scissors, markers, and other art modalities to meet our Inner Oppressor. For this quest, I want to keep it simple and cost effective. Instead of buying every art tool under the sun, you'll use a colorful writing instrument to do the self-reflective art exercises. Get some pens, markers, crayons, or pencil crayons. You'll need at least three different colors. If you can get more colors, do so. Use what you already own, or borrow the items from your children or other little ones in your care (ask permission, of course).

A blank page has been provided for each self-reflective art activity for you to draw or doodle right in this workbook. This, again, is a simple and cost-effective way to participate in the Inner Field Trip quest. If you're like me and you don't like marking up the pages of a book, you can buy a sketchbook or journal in which to do the self-reflective art. Dollar stores and other variety stores sell inexpensive notebooks or sketchbooks for a few dollars or less. There is no need to purchase a high-grade art journal, as that would be beyond the scope of this quest. Another option is to use the cardboard boxes that items you have ordered have been shipped in. Instead of putting the boxes out for recycling, you can cut or tear them into smaller pieces and use them to do your art.*

No matter the materials you use, just remember that what you're producing during the self-reflective arts portion of the Inner Field Trip isn't something that is to be sold, judged, critiqued, or graded. The self-reflective art you produce during the Inner Field Trip will be unrefined, expressive, rough, unpolished, and simple. You do not need to be an artist or have artistic ability to engage in self-reflective arts activities. You simply need to be curious.

Journaling Tools

You can choose to journal using pen and paper or keyboard and screen. There are benefits and drawbacks to both approaches. In my workshops, attendees use pen and paper to journal, and I love seeing people giving their hands a quick massage or shaking their arms after writing for a few minutes. With pen and paper, there's a somatic and tactile experience. The somatic experience of handwriting helps to build a connection between the body and both hemispheres of the brain. One study showed that a wider area of the brain was activated when participants used handwriting to create words and drawings on a page.** Another benefit to using pen and paper is that handwriting forces you to slow down and take your time.

If you use pen and paper, you can purchase a journal specifically for the Inner Field Trip. If getting a journal does not sound appealing, you can, instead, buy loose-leaf lined paper and a clipboard or binder. Pens are also

---

* If you go to the Inner Field Trip channel on YouTube, you'll find a tutorial where I offer some other materials on which you can do your art, especially if you're under-resourced financially, can't get to the store, or want to do the self-reflective art on a more challenging surface.

** van der Meer, Audrey L. H., and F. R. van der Weel. "Only Three Fingers Write, but the Whole Brain Works: A High-Density EEG Study Showing Advantages of Drawing Over Typing for Learning." *Frontiers in Psychology* 8 (May 2017). https://doi: 10.3389/fpsyg.2017.00706.

especially important. Choose a pen and paper combination that won't interrupt your flow of thoughts. Nothing is more irritating than using a pen that leaks as you write or paper that is too rough under the hand or too bright for the eyes. Today, Day 5, would be the day to test out a few paper and pen combinations so you're ready for Part 2, which starts on Day 8.

Using a keyboard and screen is also a good way to journal. Some patrons find that typing is better, as they can keep up with the ramblings of their Inner Oppressor. There are several options that you can use to journal digitally. I won't list specific apps or websites, as there are so many.* What I will recommend is that you use a note-taking or word-processing app where the cursor moves down the page as you type so you don't have to scroll. It's a small thing, yet it's one less action you'll need to perform while typing.

What if you don't like to journal? Some don't write or type for various reasons. If that's you, voice journaling is an option. You can speak into the microphone on your handheld device or computer, then use an app to turn your spoken words into text. If you choose to voice journal, be sure that you can record in private. Whatever your Inner Oppressor reveals to you is between you and your Inner Oppressor.

If you don't want to record your voice journal, you can speak quietly to yourself. The drawback of this approach is that you won't have a recorded account of what your Inner Oppressor has revealed (you'll see why having the writings is important in Part 3). However, if recording your voice journal using an app doesn't work for you, mutter softly out loud instead. You can treat it as if you're praying to the Creator.

Your Actions

Step 1—Identify your mood before starting. Go to page 239 and use the Mood Tracker to capture how you're feeling.

Step 2—Start collecting the art and journaling tools you'll need to participate in the Inner Field Trip. Once you've collected what you need, do a dry run so you can test out how the instruments feel in your hands.

---

* Check the Inner Field Trip YouTube channel for a list of apps I've used to journal.

Step 3—Organize the items. Put them in a dedicated backpack, reusable bag, or box so you're not scrambling to find things once you sit in your cozy grotto.

Step 4—Track your mood after completing the Guided Self-Reflective Activities. Go to page 239 and use the Mood Tracker to capture how you're feeling now that you're done.

Congratulations!

You have completed today's actions. Please resist the urge to move quickly to the next day's actions. If you have capacity, you can also file your Summary Report at https://summary.innerfieldtrip.com (optional). Otherwise, go to page 243 and color in the day that you completed on the Journey Tracker page, put the Inner Field Trip aside, get on with your day, then resume tomorrow at the time you booked to meet with your Inner Oppressor.

What to Do When Your Stomach Gets Queasy

*E*xploring unconscious biases has an effect, not only on your relationships but also on your body. In the years I've guided patrons and workshop attendees through the Inner Field Trip quest, many have reported physical symptoms that leave them feeling exhausted and irritated. Heaviness in the chest. Knots in the stomach. Increased fatigue. Lack of appetite. Tightness in the throat. Strange dreams. These somatic and physical responses cause some to abandon the Inner Field Trip quest because it hurts their bodies so much.

After doing self-reflective journaling, one workshop attendee, Adam, who was once talkative, had become pensive and quiet. After a few people spoke, Adam put up his hand. In a restrained, measured voice, he said:

> I grew up in a small suburb. I remember feeling as if I were growing up on a movie set. My parents and the people in my community were the actors playing a role. I couldn't talk to anybody about how I felt. Connecting the dots to the dominant culture and why I believed the lies makes me angry. I did not ask to be part of a system that does so much damage to people. Yes, I have privilege and I don't feel I have the right to express the kind of pain that the People of Color in this room are expressing. But I'm mad about the lies. What friendships have I been denied because I believed a lie?

The intensity of emotions that will emerge while going through Days 8–25 will leave you confused and your body in a state of turmoil. Your Inner

Oppressor will try to resist what's happening. It will sing you a sweet song of returning to the status quo. Once you begin the Guided Self-Reflective Activities in Part 2, you will start to feel a little weird. One or more of the symptoms I described on the previous page will happen. You can expect this to occur after you've done the first three to four days in Part 2. You'll feel the need to withdraw or take a break. You'll want to disappear.

I call this "Journey Fatigue." The Guided Self-Reflective Activities feel like an attack on your nervous system. Your anxieties will be activated, and you will feel utterly overstimulated. Contempt will build. You'll direct it towards me, your Inner Oppressor, or someone close to you. Maybe all of the above!

One way to navigate through Journey Fatigue is to know that it's an expected part of this process. You are shedding, emptying, and questioning. Part of what you'll uncover are the mistruths and false narratives you've been led to believe about your social, ethnic, biological, or behavioral identities (SEBBIs). You'll grieve what you didn't know and the ways you upheld systems of oppression. You'll be sad about the loss of an identity, even if you now know that identity was false.

The sadness, anger, disbelief, and bargaining are the emotions that appear in the stages of grieving.* If you are trying to reclaim your humanity, then you have every right to feel these emotions. They are not signs of fragility.** You're not using your emotions to shut down, suppress, or silence conversations around unconscious biases or systemic oppression. The emotions that emerge as you're going through the Inner Field Trip are ones that reflect the grief you're feeling deep in your body and soul (you'll learn more about this on Day 26).

The best way to combat Journey Fatigue is to put together what I call an "Endurance Kit." Hikers carry first-aid kits to handle emergencies as soon as they occur. If a hiker experiences an injury or gets lost, a first-aid kit contains materials to help contain the emergency as quickly as possible. The "injuries" you'll experience while going on an Inner Field Trip will be different from the

---

* The stages of grieving were first introduced in 1969 by Dr. Elisabeth Kübler-Ross in her book *On Death and Dying*. She spent the rest of her career correcting the false assumption that the stages happen one at a time and are time limited. Instead, Dr. Kübler-Ross stated that the stages can all happen at the same time and can last several days, weeks, or even years.

** "White fragility" is a term coined by Dr. Robin DiAngelo to name the intense emotions white people experience when they are exposed to conversations about racism. As this is a book about exploring unconscious biases, and not just skin-color advantages, I'm using the more generic term "fragility."

ones you'll experience if you're hiking. But just like a hiker, identifying what you'll add to your Endurance Kit will help you move through Journey Fatigue so you can continue meeting your Inner Oppressor.

Here are some ideas on what you should include in your Endurance Kit:

Understand that it's a part of the process. You are exploring generations of unconscious biases, and you may very well be the first in your bloodline to interrogate your lineage's complicity to the dominant culture. Some of your ancestors will be pleased that someone is finally doing this work; others will be quite upset.

Let those close to you know what you're doing. Although you'll do the Inner Field Trip on your own, it's a good idea to inform your inner circle that you may need help. Arrange childcare, eldercare, or pet care for your loved ones. If your loved ones are supportive, ask your partner or roommates to pick up chores (and make sure to tell them you will do the same for them if they decide to embark on this journey after you complete your quest).

Your inner circle can be friends, family, chosen family, or a therapist. Self-reliance is a trait of the dominant culture, making you believe that you need to do things on your own. You cannot do this work alone even though you're doing this work alone. As you go on the Inner Field Trip, let those close to you know what to expect. This is like returning from a hike with muddy boots. Tell them to expect that as you enter the front door, the mud will mess up the floor. Ask them to help you clean up. In other words, ask whoever you trust to hold space for you as you end each day of the Inner Field Trip with your proverbial muddy boots.

Engage in Active Rest Stops. Whenever I hike, I often take a 5–10 minute break for every 60–75 minutes of hiking to eat a snack, review the trail map, and drink some water. I'm not pitching a tent and throwing open a sleeping bag so I can settle in for the night; I'm simply taking a quick break before continuing. Active Rest Stops are added to the Inner Field Trip so you can, as Resmaa Menakem writes in *My Grandmother's Hands*, discharge trapped energy. You'll learn more about Active Rest Stops in Part 2 on Day 11.

Talk to a mental health professional. A small percentage of those who go on an Inner Field Trip find that it activates memories that are too troubling to process on their own. Some patrons in my community will go on an Inner Field Trip, then schedule time to speak with their therapist. If you have access to a mental health professional or have been planning to engage with one, you can work through unresolved issues that come up during the Inner Field Trip. Remember that even if those closest to you are offering their full support, some issues may arise that only a trained professional can help you heal from.

Join the Inner Field Trip Basecamp. You'll be navigating a very different perspective than those held by your family members or inner circle of friends. In cases such as this, you will not only be dealing with what confronting your Inner Oppressor brings up for you but also how it will impact the way you see the choices and actions of those close to you. You will need help in deciding how to move forward with that knowledge, especially if you can't be totally honest with those whom you are closest to.

If your support circle is too small, nonexistent, or too far away, the good news is that you can join the Inner Field Trip Basecamp. Each month, the Inner Field Trip Licensed Navigators, who have been trained by me, lead sessions that nourish and rejuvenate. Licensed Navigators also lead a 30-day Inner Field Trip challenge in a cohort format for those who have bought the workbook and need to do the quest with others. In between challenges, Brave Trekkers participate in Fireside Chats. These are community forums that are private, judgment-free, and supportive. Some even form small groups in their local communities to offer in-person peer support in homes, parks, coffee shops, and other public places. The Inner Field Trip Basecamp is a place where you can land softly as you stumble along bravely. Visit basecamp.innerfieldtrip .com to learn how to join.

Your Actions

Step 1—Identify your mood before starting. Go to page 239 and use the Mood Tracker to capture how you're feeling.

Step 2—Identify who or what to include in your Endurance Kit. If you need to send up an emergency flare, who or what would be the best to support you?

Step 3—Fill in the blanks below. I will manage Journey Fatigue by:

_____

_____

_____

_____

_____

_____

Step 4—Track your mood after completing the Guided Self-Reflective Activities. Go to page 239 and use the Mood Tracker to capture how you're feeling now that you're done.

Congratulations!

You have completed today's actions. Please resist the urge to move quickly to the next day's actions. If you have capacity, you can also file your Summary Report at https://summary.innerfieldtrip.com (optional). Otherwise, go to page 243 and color in the day that you completed on the Journey Tracker page, put the Inner Field Trip aside, get on with your day, then resume tomorrow at the time you booked to meet with your Inner Oppressor.

What to Do If You Miss a Day or Two (or More)

I try to hike at least three to four times a week. Some weeks, I hit that goal. Other weeks, I don't go hiking at all. For the weeks where I do not hike, I don't try to catch up. It's impossible to do three to four 2-hour hikes in one day to make up for the days I missed. Instead, I simply start where I am.

You may find that after taking inventory of your identities (Day 1), deciding who you're becoming (Day 2), scheduling a can't-miss meeting with you Inner Oppressor (Day 3), creating your cozy grotto (Day 4), gathering the tools (Day 5), and packing an Endurance Kit to combat Journey Fatigue (Day 6), you may miss a day or two (or more) as you continue through the rest of the Inner Field Trip quest.

With all that planning, you may feel guilty about missing a day or two (or more), especially if you are from a Historically Desired Group (HDG) and know that people from Historically Undesired Groups (HUGs) cannot withdraw from identity-based oppression by choice or because their lives are otherwise busy, and they don't "have time" to be oppressed today. If you succumb to guilt and despair about your missed days, you may feel tempted to catch up by doing two, three, or more chapters in one sitting so you don't fall behind. But this is not a race.

When I used to host multi-day challenges once a quarter for my patrons, some would use the weekend to rush through two or more prompts. Then, they'd ashamedly report on the last day of the quest that after trying to work through so many prompts at once, they could not complete the rest of the Inner Field Trip.

Let me first assure you that you're not falling behind if you miss a day or more. If that happens, just pick up where you left off and continue with the quest. Trying to rush through several Guided Self-Reflective Activities is one of the traits of the dominant culture—that of hyper-achievement and competition rather than taking time to reflect and contemplate. Urgency is one trait (of many) that you're trying to unpack as you continue the Inner Field Trip.

Statistically, it's impossible to catch up. Doing the Inner Field Trip for one hour a day can't compete with the rest of the hours that the dominant culture uses to keep you attached to the status quo. Don't believe me? Let's look at this simple equation. If everyone has 24 hours in a day, then we all have 168 hours in a week (24 hours x 7 days). If we subtract the average hours of sleep a week that adults in North America get (7 hours per night x 7 days = 49 hours), then we're left with 119 waking hours. If we subtract the number of hours per week spent on the Inner Field Trip (1 hour per day x 7 days = 7 hours), then the remaining 112 hours are used by the dominant culture to expose you to its beliefs.

How does the dominant culture do this?

- It uses films and television shows to display people from HDGs as the victors and heroes and people from HUGs as villains and victims.

- It ensures that books are written by people from HDGs on a wide variety of topics and restricts most people from HUGs to writing books only in certain categories.

- It ensures that workplace practices reflect the attitudes of people from HDGs and diminishes people from HUGs to less visible and less paid positions, especially when HUGs dare to acknowledge these double standards, biases, or diminishments.

- It uses the media (and even politicians with large platforms) to reinforce that people from HUGs are to blame for their plight in life.

- It uses history to show that people from HDGs did all these great things and everyone else did the opposite or was simply "invisible."

After reading how the dominant culture commandeers your remaining waking hours, you may be feeling, "Well, what's the point?" The point is that you must start somewhere. While you cannot undo the centuries of unconscious biases passed on to you from your ancestors by catching up, you are doing what no one else in your bloodline had the courage (or resources, depending on your ancestry) to do.

Eventually, as the Inner Field Trip becomes a habit, one that you do each day for the rest of your life, your waking hours become less anchored in the lessons of the dominant culture and more grounded in the lessons of liberation and healing. Your one hour of Inner Field Trip activity today may become five hours of pro-human, pro-liberation, pro-healing actions tomorrow. One person doing the Inner Field Trip today can influence 10 people tomorrow who then go on to influence 100. Then, several generations from now, millions of our descendants will look back and thank you and me for being the first to pass on healing and not pain. You will most likely adopt the words of Myisha T. Hill, author of *Heal Your Way Forward*:

I'm not anti-anything. I believe in collective liberation. I believe in common humanity. I'm pro-liberation, pro-healing, pro-justice, pro-wholeness, pro-growth, pro-abolition. Yea all that!

If you miss a day or two, brush yourself off and rejoin the quest wherever you left off. Remember, you are not falling behind. You are not missing out. You will not be scolded or chastised because you missed a day or more. Start where you are. What you're doing at this moment is enough.

Your Actions

Step 1—Identify your mood before starting. Go to page 239 and use the Mood Tracker to capture how you're feeling.

Step 2—Fill in the blanks. Here is the way I will be gentle with myself if I miss a day or two (or more):

_____

_____

_____

_____

Step 3—Track your mood after completing the Guided Self-Reflective Activities. Go to page 239 and use the Mood Tracker to capture how you're feeling now that you're done.

Congratulations!

You have completed today's actions. Please resist the urge to move quickly to the next day's actions. If you have capacity, you can also file your Summary Report at https://summary.innerfieldtrip.com (optional). Otherwise, go to page 243 and color in the day that you completed on the Journey Tracker page, put the Inner Field Trip aside, get on with your day, then resume tomorrow at the time you booked to meet with your Inner Oppressor.

PART

2

During the Quest

After parking my car, I jump out, grab my backpack, and walk towards the trailhead (also known as the start of the trail). I can feel the excitement rising in my heart and body as I start off on my hike. There's a lightness in each of my steps and a feeling of joy as I anticipate the journey ahead. With a backpack filled with supplies and the confidence I feel about all the preparation I've done, I'm ready for whatever awaits me as I explore the trail.

You're most likely feeling excited, happy, giddy, anxious, and nervous about the quest ahead. Days 8–25 are the days where you will explore some of the traits of the dominant culture. You'll use the Guided Self-Reflective Activities to meet your Inner Oppressor and finally identify how the traits of the dominant culture live within you.

Before turning the page to begin Day 8, I want to remind you that the excitement you feel won't last. Eventually, Journey Fatigue will set in. That's why Active Rest Stops have been added after every three to four days of the quest to remind you to take a mindful break. It's vitally important that you use Active Rest Stops to recover before moving on to the next day's activities.

Are you ready? Let's move to Day 8.

Meet Your Inner Oppressor

*E*arlier in this book, you learned a little bit about the Inner Oppressor. Now it's time to meet that part of you that bullies and pressures you to submit to and obey the dominant culture. Your Inner Oppressor acts the way it does to keep you safe, secure, and socially supported. As such, you cannot conquer, eliminate, overcome, silence, trick, defeat, fight, or banish your Inner Oppressor. If systems of oppression exist, so, too, will your Inner Oppressor.

In some ways, the Inner Oppressor sounds like the Inner Critic.* Both are shaped by lived experiences and family programming, and both operate to help you avoid pain, suffering, and rejection. Despite these similarities, there are profound differences between the two. While your Inner Critic will convince you that no one likes you, your Inner Oppressor says no one likes you due to your social, ethnic, biological, and behavioral identities (SEBBIs), or reinforces you, if you are a member of a favored group, in adopting critical attitudes towards others who are not "like you." Another key difference between the two is that your Inner Critic will convince you that you'll never succeed, while your Inner Oppressor says that you'll never succeed due to systemic oppression and

---

* Sigmund Freud and Carl Jung, both early contributors to psychotherapy, are credited with the concept of the Inner Critic. Since then, others have conceptualized that part of us that constantly fills our inner dialogue with negative messaging. Although some have used terms such as "internalized oppression," "self-imposed oppression," and "subjugated self" to refer to how we self-suppress and self-marginalize, including W. E. B. Du Bois who wrote about minority consciousness, I haven't seen anyone use the term "Inner Oppressor." While I'd like to take credit for coining the phrase, "Inner Oppressor" is a term that builds upon the work of earlier thinkers and theorists.

structural barriers, or—even more damagingly—that you won't succeed because those different from you, such as immigrants, for example, are going to steal your job and the success that is your birthright as a member of the dominant cultural group. Your Inner Critic operates in the here and now, while your Inner Oppressor uses intergenerational messages from the past to influence your behaviors today, so you don't plan for the future.

Your Inner Oppressor sounds dystopian, doesn't it? Yet, it's so important to meet it so you understand what drives you to align with the Culture of the DEAD, one that **d**ehumanizes, **e**xploits, **a**buses, and **d**ominates those subjected to identity-based oppression. The opposite of being awake, conscious, or attentive is being unaware, unconscious, or inattentive. Where there is no life, there is death. There is no in between. If you are striving to be a better ancestor and create a culture that celebrates diverse and interesting people, meeting your Inner Oppressor is one of the most alive things you can do.

Inner Oppressor Examples

Later in this chapter, you'll have a chance to draw your Inner Oppressor, give it a name, then capture its ramblings through journaling. Before meeting your Inner Oppressor, it may be helpful to understand how others have reacted after seeing a visual representation of theirs. In workshops that I've led both online and in person, I invite attendees to draw their Inner Oppressor. I'm often surprised at how quickly they complete the exercise. No one complains about not being able to draw. Instead, they put pen to paper and render an image within a few short minutes.

In workshop rooms, attendees will only have access to a pen or pencil plus a notebook. When I lead these sessions online, attendees typically have access to markers, pencil crayons, pastels, and crayons in multiple colors. As result, some Inner Oppressor drawings are simple while others are more detailed. Whatever instrument you choose to draw your Inner Oppressor, don't spend too much time on it. It's better to use a pen and create a simple drawing in five minutes or less than to use 10 different colors and spend hours laboring over the drawing.

You can visit www.inneroppressor.com to see videos and photos of Inner Oppressors submitted by patrons and workshop attendees. I'm sharing some in this chapter for inspiration. Riley, a nonbinary patron, drew their Inner Oppressor, *Anxious Annabelle*, symbolized as a child and had to this to say of her:

She's loud, needs attention, everything that happens to her is a tragedy, no one else matters because she's uncomfortable—it goes on. Part of me wants to protect her from feeling anything bad, but I know her tears are false and meant to draw me away from important things. If I join her in the blanket fort away from everything that's uncomfortable, that's just what she wants.

Some draw their Inner Oppressor in the form of a woman. Reegan, a patron who calls her Inner Oppressor *Pinned Down Penelope*, wrote this after reflecting on her drawing:

Pinned Down Penelope is isolated, withdrawn, and shut off from the world in every way—alone, headphones, lights out, blinds drawn, Netflix, phone, wine, pills, a stack of unread books to the side. Her intentions are there with the books, but intentions are worth NOTHING without action. They are tokenizing and virtue signaling. When my Inner Oppressor is in this place, she's useless. I feel like my Inner Oppressor wants me to be pinned in this bed feeling powerless and overwhelmed.

Others, like Danté, drew their Inner Oppressor as a man. Here's what Danté had to say about *Fragile Francis*:

Say hello to Fragile Francis. Francis cannot bear to be told that his behavior is harmful because that would shatter the enormously fragile conception of himself. Rather than face the consequences of his behavior, Francis will cite all the ways he has been hurt over the years and center himself instead of taking any accountability. Francis will avoid, hide, neglect, and disappear rather than do the hard work of being self-reflective, apologizing without conditional "buts," and twist the story around to manipulate the person who was brave enough in the first place to bring up the harm. Fragile Francis is a master manipulator wearing a mask of "I'm too hurt inside to deal with this; please feel sorry for me."

In some cases, the Inner Oppressor is envisioned as a council or group. Each Inner Oppressor takes on a different characteristic. Here's how Kelli, a patron, described *Patty Perfection* and *Harmonious Hallie*, her Inner Oppressor twins:

Patty has a clipboard and a whistle and she's always watching. She has the list of infractions written down and she knows the rules and will blow the whistle on me when I'm not following them. Hallie requires harmony at all costs. She avoids conflict and bends over backwards to make sure there is peace. Patty hangs out on my back, looking over my right shoulder, while Hallie hangs out in the middle of my chest like a worn baby. These ladies work hard to keep me "safe."

·   ·   ·

Some envision their Inner Oppressor as a nonhuman object. I've seen some draw their Inner Oppressor as squiggly lines, large and small dots, and a power grid. Yvette's Inner Oppressor is conceptualized as a council; however, instead of drawing human beings, she drew them as masks, giving each a different name. Here's what Yvette had to say about *Frozen Frankie*, *Ignorant Ines*, and *Silencing Sam*:

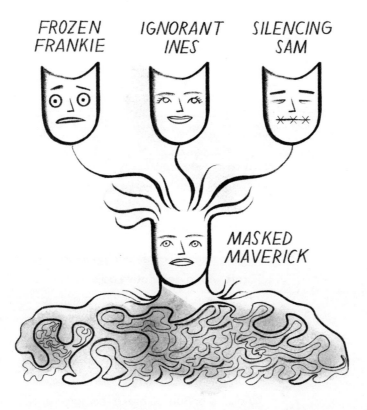

Trying to sum up my Inner Oppressor felt like trying to herd cats. Then I realized my Inner Oppressor has many faces and strategies. I immediately saw a bunch of masks in my mind's eye. So, I drew a few masks that represent the many faces of my IO. Each mask feels like it has its own damning belief system. Frozen Frankie likes to tell me that I can't handle discomfort and big feelings, so they freeze. Ignorant Ines likes to think she's beyond this and doesn't want to participate. Silencing Sam holds the beliefs of perfectionism and silences me, causing a lot of inaction.

Now that you've seen how some draw their Inner Oppressor, it's time to meet yours.

Guided Self-Reflective Activities

The best way to meet your Inner Oppressor is to draw it. Often, what cannot be conveyed through words can be best revealed through images.

Step 1—Identify your mood before starting. Go to page 239 and use the Mood Tracker to capture how you're feeling.

Step 2—Draw Your Inner Oppressor (15 minutes).

Supplies needed: Colored markers or pens, timer.

What to do:

- Set your timer to count down from 15 minutes, then draw your Inner Oppressor.
- Give your Inner Oppressor a name.

The name you give your Inner Oppressor should start with a descriptive adjective, followed by a first name. I suggest using an alliteration. In other words, whatever letter your descriptive adjective starts with (for example, an A for apathetic or an S for suffocating), choose a first name with that same letter (for example, Agatha or Sue) to make the name even more memorable.

Examples include Destructive Delores, Suffocating Sue, Controlling Connor, Judgmental Jen, Punishing Power Grid, Bound Bonnie, Soul-Stealer Sludge, Scared Susan, Angry Adam, Sneaky Seth, Vanishing Void, just to name a few.

If your IO has an alter ego, give them both names. Examples include Dismissive Debbie and Defensive Danielle, or Unquestioning Ursula and Angry Adam.

Use the space below to draw your Inner Oppressor.

Step 3—Journal (15 minutes).

Supplies needed: Sketchbook or journal, pen/pencil OR keyboard and screen, timer.

What to do:

- Navigate the prompt using GPS (see page 237).
- Set your timer to count down from 15 minutes.
- Capture the ramblings of your Inner Oppressor using the following prompts as a guide:

Prompt #1: What motivates your Inner Oppressor (IO)? What is your IO trying to protect you from? What's your IO so afraid of anyways?

Prompt #2: What social, ethnic, biological, or behavioral (SEBBIs) did you choose to represent your Inner Oppressor? What do the SEBBIs of your IO tell you about who you believe upholds power in systems of oppression?

Prompt #3: Does seeing your Inner Oppressor produce any physical sensations? What do these physical cues tell you about the way your IO affects your body? How does knowing this help you understand the link between physical/mental wellness and systemic biases, especially for marginalized and oppressed groups?

Step 4—Track your mood after completing the Guided Self-Reflective Activities. Go to page 239 and use the Mood Tracker to capture how you're feeling now that you're done.

Congratulations!

You have completed today's actions. Please resist the urge to move quickly to the next day's actions. If you have capacity, you can also file your Summary Report at https://summary.innerfieldtrip.com (optional). Otherwise, go to page 243 and color in the day that you completed on the Journey Tracker page, put the Inner Field Trip aside, get on with your day, then resume tomorrow at the time you booked to meet with your Inner Oppressor.

Explore Perfection

Before publishing this workbook, I used to publish prompts in my online community every week.* The first prompt people would work through is one focused on perfection. Most have no clue that there is a strong connection between perfection and systems of oppression. After exploring perfection using the Guided Self-Reflective Activities some develop an awareness of how much of their humanity is wrapped up in being seen as flawless, pure, immaculate, and error-free.

The dominant culture uses perfection to demand that you do everything right. People of Historically Desired Groups (HDGs) are so afraid of making a mistake that they often avoid working with anti-oppression and anti-racism groups. Patrons and workshop attendees who have worked through this prompt and identify with HDGs have said that they fear messing up and making people from Historically Undesired Groups (HUGs) angry by saying the wrong thing or acting the wrong way. After doing this prompt, many could see that perfection was stopping them from taking any action at all. One patron pensively said that perfection separates us from our voice, body, and humanity.

That is the goal of perfection. It causes you to monitor your thoughts, actions, and behaviors so you don't make a mistake. You're so busy keeping watch over your actions, you do the same thing to others. Patrons and workshop attendees have lamented the overpowering effects of perfection. The need to pursue flawless action causes many to judge themselves harshly even before they make a mistake.

The dominant culture teaches HDGs that the outcome of being imperfect is rejection. However, making mistakes has a different outcome for people of

---

* The prompts I used to publish in the online community are now available in this workbook, so you won't find them in the Inner Field Trip Basecamp.

HUGs. Some HUGs believe that if they never mess up, they'll be accepted by members of the dominant culture. Part of being perfect is to speak the dominant culture's language without an accent and practice its culture by abandoning their own. Patrons and workshop attendees lament the loss of speaking their ancestral languages, such as Spanish, Mandarin, and French Creole, due to their parents' quest to sound perfect.

While some HUGs try to be perfect* to fit in, others strive for perfection to avoid harassment, harm, or violence. A major theme for patrons and workshop attendees who identify as Black is the exhaustion they feel at being hypervigilant about the way they're acting or behaving. They are aware that their presence is enough to cause others to see them as a threat. Messing up, as a Black person, could cost them their life. This tension lives in the body and can create a variety of health issues.

What Is Possible When You Release Perfection

First, making mistakes is a key ingredient to making new things. It is impossible to dismantle systems of oppression with dominant culture thinking. As Audre Lorde wrote, "The master's tools will never dismantle the master's house."** It takes creativity, imagination, and innovation to unravel the status quo. You have to courageously write the book that has never been written, paint the art that has never been painted, compose the song that has never been sung, and develop an equitable corporate culture that has never been done before. In order to produce or create a generation-changing process, project, or product, you have to try something—and fail. And maybe fail again. Becoming a better ancestor means shunning the culture of perfection so you can create a more equitable culture.

---

* "Perfection" here is a word indicating conformity to the standards of the dominant culture, not absolute perfection, which does not exist, and which would certainly not mandate avoiding Chinese food or friends who are also of the same HUG.

** Audre Lorde (1934–1992), a womanist writer and civil rights activist, shared this quote at a conference held in New York in 1979, celebrating the 30-year anniversary of the release of Simone de Beauvoir's book *The Second Sex*. According to Lester C. Olsen, who wrote a journal article entitled "The Personal, the Political, and Others: Audre Lorde Denouncing 'The Second Sex Conference,'" Lorde admonished the conference organizers for not including more diverse voices. By not doing so, Lorde said, the conference organizers were using tools of oppression layered in patriarchy. Lorde's quote was expanded into an essay that was included in her 1984 book, *Sister Outsider: Speeches and Essays*.

Second, releasing perfection means you can extend grace to those who are trying to be and do better. Too often in social justice groups, a person is banished for making a mistake. Certainly, if the person did something illegal, performed a microaggression, or is being a bully, then, yes, they should be blocked from the group. However, there are some actions that can be considered small slights that are then blown into accusations of disrespect and the violation of one's boundaries. There's a difference, however, between someone who is trying and messes up versus someone who is not trying at all. Most who join social causes do so in an inelegant, unpolished, and awkward way. They won't know all the words, won't understand all the jargon, and may be completely ignorant to the deep history that preceded their arrival. As long as they're not trying to save, rescue, or infantilize, extend compassion when they mess up. By meeting with your Inner Oppressor through the Guided Self-Reflective Activities, you'll confront your flaws. When you see your flaws, you're better able to accept the flaws in others. In other words, we cannot use the measurement of the dominant culture to evaluate one another in social justice movements.

Lastly, perfection is anti-human. Humans are not designed to operate in error-free environments. Our brains use mistakes to adapt and grow.* Expecting one or two people within a HUG to be a perfect and flawless exception of their racial or ethnic group is unrealistic. HUGs are not a monolith and do not act, behave, or think the same, no matter what the dominant culture would have you believe. On the other hand, the lie that the dominant culture whispers to those who are from HDGs is that a function of their biology or social class makes them pure, flawless, and unblemished. If that were the case, the dark side of being human would never infiltrate your life. You wouldn't experience devastation, illness, or poverty. Do your humanity a favor and stop punishing yourself for being imperfect.

As an aside, we need to train our Inner Oppressor to aim for precision, not perfection. Being accurate is different from being free of flaws and defects. In some occupations, mistakes can have disastrous effects. People who perform surgeries, build bridges, replace the brakes on vehicles, write words, or create

---

* If you type the term "neuroscience of mistakes" in a search engine, you'll find countless journal articles and blog posts containing research on what our brain does when we make mistakes and how we benefit when we do.

and pass laws need to do their jobs carefully and correctly. Yet, humans are not machines. Demanding supreme excellence or flawlessness can do the opposite; it can create an environment of fear and secrecy. In addition, perfection means that the surgeon, engineer, mechanic, journalist, or lawmaker is so complete that they don't require supervision, professional development, or training to improve and grow. When we, instead, aim for precision, it means that we're being thoughtful about the outcome, transparent about the process, and mindful about how our actions will affect others.

Ultimately, the work of changing the dominant culture into an equitable one is lifelong work.

Guided Self-Reflective Activities

Step 1—Identify your mood before starting. Go to page 239 and use the Mood Tracker to capture how you're feeling.

Step 2—Continuous House Drawing (15 minutes).

Supplies needed: Sketchbook, colored markers or pens, timer.
What to do: ✂ Set your timer to count down from 15 minutes. ✂ Without lifting up your writing instrument, draw or doodle a picture of a house with a tree and a person standing outside the front door.

Use the space below to draw a continuous picture.

Step 3—Journal (15 minutes)

Supplies needed: Sketchbook or journal, pen/pencil OR keyboard and screen, timer.

What to do:
- Navigate the prompt using GPS (see page 237)
- Set your timer to count down from 15 minutes.
- Capture the ramblings of your Inner Oppressor in your journal or sketchbook using the following prompts as a guide:

Prompt #1: What's the opposite of perfection? No, not the dictionary meaning—your interpretation. How does the opposite of perfection make you feel? Do you want more of perfection's opposite in your life? Why or why not?

Prompt #2: What are you secretly afraid of if you give up perfection? Who will you disappoint? Why should that no longer matter to you?

Step 4—Track your mood after completing the Guided Self-Reflective Activities. Go to page 239 and use the Mood Tracker to capture how you're feeling now that you're done.

Congratulations!

You have completed today's actions. Please resist the urge to move quickly to the next day's actions. If you have capacity, you can also file your Summary Report at https://summary.innerfieldtrip.com (optional). Otherwise, go to page 243 and color in the day that you completed on the Journey Tracker page, put the Inner Field Trip aside, get on with your day, then resume tomorrow at the time you booked to meet with your Inner Oppressor.

Explore Rugged Individualism

Pull yourself up by the bootstraps. Hard work always pays off. Become a self-made millionaire. These are the messages the dominant culture uses to convince us that being industrious, busy, and self-reliant are the only ingredients to an economically rewarding life. This is known as "rugged individualism." It is rugged because the tasks are rough, taxing, and difficult. It is individual because this type of work is conducted by one person who, against all odds, achieves a measure of success due to nothing but sheer determination.

The problem with rugged individualism is that it is an ageist, classist, racist, and ableist philosophy. Although the dominant culture conditions us to believe that everyone can achieve greatness through hard work alone, the reality is that those who are able-bodied, youthful, healthy, wealthy, and hold skin-color privilege are implicitly supported by the dominant culture to get ahead. I point this out not to blame those who hold these traits, but to draw attention to which bodies are valued and which ones are not. It's easy for those from Historically Desired Groups (HDGs) to say that working hard works because they don't face a barrage of structural barriers.

For those from Historically Undesired Groups (HUGs), they and their ancestors have been working hard for generations, but due to systemic oppression and structural barriers, their work has not been valued or adequately compensated. The labor of some of my ancestors was violently extracted, stolen, and plundered on plantations in Jamaica for generations. The horrors of that life are documented, both by formerly enslaved Africans and those who owned plantations,* and detail how hard my ancestors worked with no monetary compensation. Through the system of chattel slavery that existed in the Americas from the early 1600s until the last country, Brazil, abolished it in 1898, we see the far extreme of the lie of rugged individualism. Enslaved Africans labored endlessly, generation after generation, for absolutely no reward at all, while plantation owners profited, even after emancipation.**

In our current culture, while things may not be that cut and dry, we can still see that those who do hard manual labor for long hours, such as those who work in factories or on farms, labor mightily and yet rarely do they profit in ways the HDG most values: power and economic gains. In a capitalist society, being born into wealth and into an HDG predisposes the person to thrive further under capitalism, where it often "takes money to make money," as the saying goes.

As wealth differentials between the top and the bottom of our economic groups widen ever more, many from HUGs remain trapped without genuine opportunities to elevate themselves, but many from HGDs will too often point to "exceptional" individuals (former president of the United States Barack Obama being a more recent example) to try and state that racism, for example, no longer exists since a Black man can become president.

While it is indeed progress in our culture that someone who would once have been enslaved due to skin color can rise to the presidency, that in absolutely no way means that racism no longer exists or that structural and institutional racism is no longer at work. We can see, for example, that even at the highest levels of power, a Black president was accused of not being a real American citizen. If this is the case, then how much more difficult is it to use

---

* The diary of Thomas Thistlewood (1721–1786), an English planter who lived in Jamaica and managed a plantation, documented the horrific acts he committed against those he enslaved. The pages of his diary are held by Yale University and are available for viewing online. Some historians believe that Thistlewood's treatment of enslaved Africans was *not* the exception.

** Through the Slave Compensation Act of 1837, Britain paid £20 million to white plantation owners as reparations for the loss of enslaved labor. At the time, this sum represented 40 percent of the British government's budget. The Royal Treasury announced in a since deleted tweet that the vast loan was paid back by taxpayers in 2015. The Centre for the Study of the Legacies of British Slave-Ownership has an online database containing the names of those who received compensation and the amount. I found both my Scottish and my French ancestors' names in the database. There is no record of Britain ever paying reparations to the newly emancipated Africans or their descendants.

the "bootstrap model" if one is in poverty, has less access to higher education, lives in a food desert, and so on?

Rugged individualism also ignores nontraditional ways of work. Some trade an hour of labor for money; others earn income through investments. Some do physical labor; others work at a desk. Some get a predictable salary every month, while others must hustle every day for their coin. Even in these situations, you must work with others in order to earn an income. The idea that you can ruggedly do the thing by yourself is a distraction. The dominant culture uses this tired narrative to redirect your attention from the real issue. The reality is that no matter how determined you are, no matter how many declarations you utter, no matter how many hours you put in, there are external factors that will mess up your plans.

Systems of oppression don't come crashing down due to the actions of one person. Yes, one person can provide a spark that ignites people to act; however, it takes many, many people to sustain a movement. Rosa Parks could not have boycotted the Montgomery Bus system on her own after being arrested for not giving up her seat to a white passenger in 1955.* The years-long boycott that followed Parks's arrest involved a community of people. In 1956, the United States Supreme Court upheld a lower court's ruling that the separation of passengers based on race was unconstitutional. Parks's quiet action led to lasting change, but only after a community stepped up to support her.

The dominant culture has done so much to disrupt our need for community. Our Inner Oppressor feeds us messages that we can't trust anyone and that it is better to do the work on our own in whatever messy or unrefined way. It's no wonder that when it comes to social justice movements, some believe that they can use rugged individualism to spark change, ignoring those who have been doing the work for years, if not decades. Then, with their shoulders slumped and their faces twisted up in mock pain, they rattle off the various

---

* Rosa Parks wasn't the only person who was arrested for not giving up her seat on a bus in segregated Alabama. In doing research for my family tree, I found out that Irene Morgan Kirkaldy, the grandmother of one of my cousins, was arrested in 1944 for not giving up her seat to a white passenger on a Greyhound bus en route from Baltimore to Virginia. Kirkaldy successfully took her case to the US Supreme Court and was represented by Thurgood Marshall, who would later become the first African American justice on the Supreme Court. In 1946, the high court struck down a Virginia state law requiring the separation of passengers due to race. Although my ancestor Kirkaldy is less well-known, both she and Parks were able to inspire change through individual action *and* community effort.

social justice tasks they performed in a cracking and wavering voice. Exhaustion is used as a badge of honor.

One way for you to release the need to do things roughly and raggedly on your own is to look at trees. Yes, you read that right. I did say trees. Not only does spending time amongst the trees help to reduce stress, boost energy, and improve the quality of sleep,* but trees also remind us of our interconnectedness. In his book *The Hidden Life of Trees: What They Feel, How They Communicate*, Peter Wohlleben opens with a foreword from Tim Flannery who says this about trees:

> The most astonishing thing about trees is how social they are. The trees in a forest care for each other, sometimes even going so far as to nourish the stump of a felled tree for centuries after it was cut down by feeding it sugars and other nutrients, and so keeping it alive.
>
> The reason trees share food and communicate is that they need each other. It's not surprising that isolated trees have far shorter lives than those living connected together in forests.

That's something I notice when I go hiking. All trees matter in the forest, no matter their height, age, or color. Nature shows that no matter the state of the tree, it still has value. A fallen tree becomes shelter for smaller animals and insects. Old trees reaching up to the sky provide a protective covering for young saplings taking root closer to the forest floor. Exposed roots provide direction and stability when walking up or down a hill. Whether a tree is alive, dead, old, or young, each holds a purpose. Trees are the answer we seek in our quest to let go of rugged individualism.

What Is Possible When You Release Rugged Individualism

You become more compassionate. Not only do you become aware of the systemic barriers preventing people of HUGs from achieving equality, equity,

---

* Spending time under a canopy of trees is known as forest bathing, or *shinrin-yoku* in Japanese. A great book on this topic is one written by Dr. Qing Li entitled *Forest Bathing: How Trees Can Help You Find Health and Happiness.*

and harmony, but you are also mindful that some are unable to work hard due to a lack of resources. As you replace rugged individualism with community care, you realize that no one is free unless all are free.*

You become aware of humanity's interconnectedness. We are connected to one another and the lands we live on. By slowing down and spending time with trees, you can deepen your appreciation of flora and fauna that surrounds you. This then leads to a better appreciation for Indigenous people and nations who continue to steward the lands so we can treat it better.

* This quote has been attributed to Fanny Lou Hamer (1917–1977), a voting and women's rights activist who said the phrase in a 1971 speech, and Maya Angelo (1928–2014), an African American poet who uttered the words in a 2013 television interview. Although Martin Luther King Jr. (1929–1968), an African American preacher and civil rights activist, is credited, I couldn't find evidence in the transcripts of his speeches. The closest was "Injustice anywhere is a threat to justice everywhere," which King wrote in a 1963 letter while imprisoned in a Birmingham jail. The first person to write "Until we are all free, we are none of us free" was Emma Lazarus, a Jewish American poet, in an 1883 essay entitled "Epistle to the Hebrews."

Guided Self-Reflective Activities

Step 1—Identify your mood before starting. Go to page 239 and use the Mood Tracker to capture how you're feeling.

Step 2—Wisdom of Trees (15 minutes).

Supplies needed: Sketchbook, colored markers or pens, timer.

What to do:

- Locate a tree, then engage it through your senses. Touch the trunk. Sniff the leaves. Stare at its branches. Listen to the sounds it makes. Doodle on the next page as the tree engages your senses.
- Not able to get to a tree? Here are a few options (choose one):

  Go to the Inner Field Trip channel on YouTube and look for a forest-bathing video in the playlist called "Guided Self-Reflective Sounds."

  Diffuse a woodsy essential oil, like cedarwood, Douglas fir, cypress, pine, or sandalwood, and inhale the treelike smells as you doodle.

  Sit near a houseplant and use your senses to engage with it as you doodle.

- Set your timer to count down from 15 minutes.

Use the space below to draw or doodle as you engage with a tree.

Step 3—Journal (15 minutes).

Supplies needed: Sketchbook or journal, pen/pencil OR keyboard and screen, timer.

What to do:

- Navigate the prompt using GPS (see page 237).
- Set your timer to count down from 15 minutes.
- Capture the ramblings of your Inner Oppressor in your journal or sketchbook using the following prompts as a guide:

Prompt #1: What did you learn about interconnectedness while engaging with the tree?

Prompt #2: In what ways has rugged individualism disconnected you from yourself, your community, and your dreams?

Prompt #3: Recall how your senses reacted to the tree.

Step 4—Track your mood after completing the Guided Self-Reflective Activities. Go to page 239 and use the Mood Tracker to capture how you're feeling now that you're done.

Congratulations!

You have completed today's actions. Please resist the urge to move quickly to the next day's actions. If you have capacity, you can also file your Summary Report at https://summary.innerfieldtrip.com (optional). Otherwise, go to page 243 and color in the day that you completed on the Journey Tracker page, put the Inner Field Trip aside, get on with your day, then resume tomorrow at the time you booked to meet with your Inner Oppressor.

Active Rest Stop

*I*n a survey conducted during a 10-day virtual Inner Field Trip with patrons in October 2020, 48.6 percent of respondents reported feeling a sensation in their chest and heart area, such as tightness or a rapid heartbeat, followed by queasy stomach and explosive diarrhea (31.9 percent), sensations in the jaw/mouth/throat area (30.6 percent), and problems in the head/forehead/temples (29.2 percent).* These are some of the physical sensations patrons experience while going through the Guided Self-Reflective Activities.

Why would the Inner Field Trip cause these physical symptoms to manifest? Why would meeting your Inner Oppressor through the Guided Self-Reflective Activities stimulate butterflies in the stomach, shallow breathing, tension in the neck, discomfort in the shoulders, persistent cough, a lump in the throat, and overall exhaustion?**

Giving yourself permission to feel all the feels is the primary reason why your body is exhibiting these sensations. The dominant culture has conditioned you to believe that facts and data are more important than feelings and emotions. Feelings can't be trusted; only facts matter. The dominant culture uses toxic positivity, spiritual bypassing, and gaslighting to cause us to distrust and diminish the messages our bodies use to inform us that something is wrong.

---

* A total of 144 patrons filled out an online survey containing the open-ended question "Where in your body did you feel a sensation before starting the Inner Field Trip?" with 10 nominal choices. A full explanation of the research methods can be found at www.innerfieldtrip.com.

** The information contained in this chapter is not intended or implied to be a substitute for professional medical advice. It is provided for educational purposes only. You assume full responsibility for how you choose to use this information. If there is a disagreement between the information presented in this chapter and what your physician has told you, it is more likely that your physician is correct. They have the benefit of knowing you and your medical history. Always seek the advice of your physician or other qualified healthcare provider about any questions you may have regarding a medical condition.

Sadly, your Inner Oppressor has learned that to keep you safe and secure, you need to hide your true feelings or cover up "negative" or "low vibe" ones with heaps of positivity. To finally be in a place where you can feel the unbridled expression of each emotion can be overwhelming, exhilarating, and frightening.

Feeling so much so soon and so often while journeying through the Inner Field Trip can be exhausting. Certain emotions manifest as sensations in different areas of the body. In a 2013 pioneering study, researchers mapped on the body where certain emotions show up.[*] Participants were shown an image of the body and asked to point to the spot where they felt anger, disgust, sadness, and love, just to name a few. Anger is concentrated in the arms, chest, shoulders, and head with some activation in the legs. Anxiety is concentrated in the torso, while surprise is clustered in the head. This explains why, when you feel anger, your head starts pounding, or when you feel fear, there's heaviness in your chest. There is a scientific explanation for the somatic reactions happening in your body.

These somatic reactions are your body informing you that you need to take a moment to catch your breath. Trying to rush through the Inner Field Trip is a recipe for emotional, mental, and physical burnout. As adrienne maree brown reminds us, pleasure is a form of activism where we do "the work . . . to reclaim our whole, happy, and satisfiable selves from the impacts, delusions, and limitations of oppression and/or supremacy."[**] Keeping this in mind, it's time to focus your attention on creative, pleasurable, and fun activities. That's what you'll do during the Active Rest Stop.

What Is an Active Rest Stop

Whenever I hike, I often take a 5–10 minute break for every 75–90 minutes of hiking. During this short period of rest, I'll eat some snacks, review the trail map, and take a moment to take in the sights and sounds of nature. Although I'm resting, it's also active. I'm not pitching a tent and throwing open a

---

[*] Nummenmaa, Lauri, Enrico Glerean, Riitta Hari, and Jari K. Hietanen. "Bodily Maps of Emotions." *Psychological and Cognitive Sciences* 111, no. 2 (November 2013): 646–651. https://doi.org/10.1073/pnas.1321664111.

[**] brown, adrienne maree. *Pleasure Activism: The Politics of Feeling Good.* Chico, CA: AKPress (2019): 13.

sleeping bag so I can settle in for the night. Instead, I'm taking a break long enough to boost my energy so I can reach the summit or lookout and journey back to my car before I lose sunlight. Pacing myself is key so I can stick with the task at hand.

This is the same with the Inner Field Trip. As you have learned, feeling so much so soon and so often can bring on exhaustion. Left unchecked, it can develop into "Journey Fatigue" (a term referring to the feeling of contempt, rage, or nervousness that emerges after participating in the Inner Field Trip for a few days with no rest). When Journey Fatigue sets in, you may abandon the Inner Field Trip once and for all. If you want to become a better ancestor and leave a legacy for generations to come, you cannot let Journey Fatigue cause you to opt out.

Journey Fatigue can be inspired by the interactions you're having with your Inner Oppressor. At times, your Inner Oppressor resists you by not revealing anything when you do the Guided Self-Reflective Activities; other times, it unloads a torrent of words that you aren't fast enough to capture. An Active Rest Stop can help you look forward to meeting your Inner Oppressor when you return to the Guided Self-Reflective Activities. If play helps couples rekindle the romance, an Active Rest Stop can help ignite your anticipation of being in communion with your Inner Oppressor once again.

The Active Rest Stop is also needed to release trapped energy in your body. This is the primary reason why trying to chisel away at the unconscious biases that have calcified and hardened in your mind, body, and soul can be shocking to you and your Inner Oppressor. Resmaa Menakem wrote about this in his book *My Grandmother's Hands*:

> After you have been in the heat of a conflict, its energy remains bottled up in your body. For your physical and emotional well-being, discharge it as soon as you reasonably can. Allow yourself to experience your body's natural defensive and protective urges—and then discharge them.

What to Do During an Active Rest Stop

Active Rest Stops are built into the 30-day Inner Field Trip quest and take place every three to four days. You'll encounter one on Days 11, 15, 20, and 25.

On these days, instead of reviewing the art or writings you produced during the previous three or four days, you will focus on creating, building, composing, moving, or making. Resmaa Menakem recommends discharging and dispersing energy nurtured through conflict or high-stress situations using movement, such as dance, playing sports, exercise, or physical labor.[*] Movement is also encouraged during the Active Rest Stop. So, too, are creative and artistic pursuits. The following infographic gives some ideas on what you can do during the Active Rest Stop:

ACTIVE REST STOP IDEAS

COMPOSE/WRITE IT
MUSIC. SCREENPLAY. MEMOIR. PANDEMIC REFLECTIONS. CREATIVE WRITING. TV SCRIPT. ONE-PERSON SHOW. PLAY

BUILD IT
BUILDING BLOCKS. POPSICLE STICKS. TOOTHPICKS. GLUE GUN. MODEL TOY. JIGSAW PUZZLE. SLIME. PLAY-DOH. MIMETIC SAND

MOVE IT
WALKING. HIKING. DANCING. CYCLING. TRAMPOLINING. SKATING. EXERCISING

MAKE IT
KNITTING. SEWING. CROCHETING. NEEDLEPOINT. EMBROIDERY. BEADING. WOODWORKING. BAKING

REFLECT ON IT
MEDITATING. PRAYING. NAPPING. DEEP BREATHING. LISTENING TO CALM MUSIC. YOGA. BUBBLE BATHING

ILLUSTRATE IT
PAINTING. DRAWING. CARTOONING. COLLAGING. JUNK JOURNALING. DIAMOND PAINTING. LETTERING

The font may be a bit small, so I've listed the six categories and related activities below:

✂ **Build It**—Building Blocks, Popsicle Sticks, Toothpicks, Glue Gun, Model Toy, Jigsaw Puzzle, Slime, Play-Doh, Mimetic Sand

---

[*] Menakem, Resmaa. *My Grandmother's Hands: Racialized Trauma and the Pathway to Mending Our Hearts and Bodies*. Las Vegas: Central Recovery Press (2017): Chapter 12.

- **Make It**—Knitting, Sewing, Crocheting, Needlepoint, Embroidery, Beading, Woodworking, Baking

- **Illustrate It**—Painting, Drawing, Cartooning, Collaging, Junk Journaling, Diamond Painting, Lettering

- **Compose/Write It**—Music, Screenplay, Memoir, Pandemic Reflections, Creative Writing, TV Script, One-Person Show, Play, Poetry

- **Move It**—Walking, Hiking, Dancing, Cycling, Trampolining, Skating, Exercising

- **Reflect on It**—Meditating, Praying, Napping, Deep Breathing, Listening to Calm Music, Yoga, Bubble Bathing, Playing Calm Music on an Instrument

Some things to remember when engaging in an Active Rest Stop:

- You're not doing this to be seen, published, or applauded. In other words, let go of any expectation of what your creation could become. Just be in the creating mood.

- It's best to do the activity solo, but if you want to include someone, choose someone with the most childlike personality. You don't want to do this with someone who's going to descend into criticism or complaints (whether directed at you or themselves).

- The activity you choose for the Active Rest Stop can be the same one you do during the next one, or totally different.

- Set the timer for 30 minutes and then let your creativity take over. Color outside the lines. Leave the mess on the floor. Play a wrong note. Write using run-on sentences. Use your nondominant hand to paint. Create a clay tree with red bark and purple leaves. Enjoy the messiness of the activity and release perfection.

Active Rest Stop Activities

Step 1—Identify your mood before starting. Go to page 239 and use the Mood Tracker Ring to capture how you are feeling.

Step 2—Engage in the Active Rest Stop (30 minutes).

Supplies needed: Materials to engage in the Active Rest Stop, timer.
What to do: ✂ Choose one Active Rest Stop activity. ✂ Take a few minutes to set up your play or studio space. ✂ Start the timer for 30 minutes, then engage in the activity until the timer goes off.

Step 3—Fill in the blanks. Once the timer goes off and before tidying up your play or studio space, complete the sentences below. Spend no more than 15 seconds on each question and jot down some thoughts.

After engaging in the Active Rest Stop, my Inner Oppressor revealed:

_____

_____

_____

_____

It's no wonder because:

_____

_____

_____

_____

Therefore, the one action I will take is:

_____

_____

_____

_____

Step 4—Track your mood after completing the Guided Self-Reflective Activities. Go to page 239 and use the Mood Tracker Ring to capture how you're feeling now that you're done.

Congratulations!

You have completed today's actions. Please resist the urge to move quickly to the next day's actions. If you have capacity, you can also file your Summary Report at https://summary.innerfieldtrip.com (optional). Otherwise, go to page 243 and color in the day that you completed on the Journey Tracker page, put the Inner Field Trip aside, get on with your day, then resume tomorrow at the time you booked to meet with your Inner Oppressor.

Explore Anti-Blackness

Anti-Blackness is a global issue* and can be defined as unprovoked and unwarranted harassment, abuse, hostility, and violence directed towards people who are African or of African descent.** It is a false narrative that people of African descent are more dangerous, violent, and aggressive due to nothing more than the color of their skin. Why some humans become dangerous is based on a complex set of economic, emotional, social, psychological, situational, and cultural factors. Being born with a darker shade of skin does not presuppose a person to a life of crime or violence. Yet, these are the incredibly racist beliefs that some hold towards people of African descent.

What is more insidious is that some will say that they don't see color,*** or they don't see race, but only the human race in an attempt to be benevolent. This sort of philosophy is often based on the idea held in most settler colonial nations, such as the United States, Canada, New Zealand, Australia, and Latin American and Caribbean countries, that immigrants are technically welcomed in these nations. It is assumed that they will assimilate to white European values and behaviors, and therefore their race will be "irrelevant." Although

---

* While there are other types of race, ethnic, religious, and ethno-religious hate, such as anti-Indigeneity, anti-Asianism, Islamophobia, and anti-Semitism, I'm focusing specifically on anti-Blackness because I am a person of African descent who will face individuals not used to being taught or led by a Black woman. By focusing on anti-Blackness, I'm not saying that other forms of race, ethnic, religious, or ethno-religious hate are irrelevant. Focus does not mean exclusion.

** Many people of African descent do not use the word "Black" to describe themselves, nor do they see their skin color as a heritage. Most will use their country of origin to describe their heritage or ancestry, such as Trinidadian, Sudanese, Brazilian, Canadian, or African American. When in doubt, ask instead of using the blanket term "Black."

*** There are some who are color-blind due to a medical condition. However, to claim color-blindness to show tolerance and acceptance is not only ableist but also racist.

people who say that they don't see color intend to show that they are not prejudiced, they are tacitly stating that as long as people "act white," they will be accepted. Even in countries anchored in a policy of multiculturalism (e.g., Canada and Australia) as opposed to a melting pot (e.g., the United States), the expectation is that immigrants would abandon their culture. Anyone who does not assimilate is seen as problematic or hostile rather than them having a right to honor their culture of origin.

To claim to be "color-blind" is a toxic way of invalidating the cultures of immigrants and People of Color. This is especially problematic for people of African descent, as our ancestors did not voluntarily choose to relocate to the Americas. They did not go to a travel agent in Lagos, Nigeria, book passage on a five-star cruise, and sit comfortably in an air-conditioned state cabin as they excitedly anticipated their arrival in Bridgetown, Barbados; Charleston, South Carolina; or Buenos Aires, Argentina. Instead, Africans were abducted, trafficked across the Atlantic, and enslaved on plantations and in both private and public spaces in Canada, the United States, Latin America, and the Caribbean. Despite this history, Black people in settler colonial countries are still expected to just emulate the behaviors, culture, and mode of speaking of their oppressors.

Beliefs lead to action. This is why some use spiritual bypassing, a method to blame bad fortunes on a lack of faith. In nonreligious circles, this may be referred to as "manifesting." Yet isn't it funny how beliefs and behaviors are connected when you want something good, but suddenly they aren't related when it comes to identity-based oppression? Black people cannot just "manifest" a life in which there is no such thing as racism.

Structural barriers and systemic oppression are driven by groups of individuals who think the same way and believe the same things. Even if a single person has stereotypical views about Africans and people of African descent, that individual is part of a family, neighborhood, workplace, or church that often "normalizes" racism. Homogeneous groups may gather in the home, at parks, in offices, and in other spaces where they make decisions about who is included and excluded.

If racist stereotypes are held by only one person in a group, that person may be called out or educated to think differently. However, the more individuals in a group who hold similar ingrained beliefs, the more likely it is that this mode of thinking will become part of that group's culture. When that kind of "groupthink" happens, individuals will not be called out or challenged for racism. For example, many who become police officers do so to do good in their communities. However, the prevalence of racism within police culture has made it difficult for those who oppose biases due to skin color to gain traction or change the tenor of the group. This is how systemic racism takes root. If many individuals within a company, organization, or group hold racist views, these beliefs influence how Black people are treated by members within that grouping.

While some groups are explicit about who they're excluding and why, others are more subtle. For example, Canada, my country of birth, enacted a whites-only immigration policy from the year of dominion in 1867 to 1968 when Prime Minister Pierre Elliott Trudeau,* the 15th prime minister of Canada, established a policy of multiculturalism that removed all discriminatory clauses from the Immigration Act. Looking back at Canada's immigration policy, you won't find the words "whites-only" written anywhere. Instead, you'll find words such as "head tax," "climate incompatibility," and "continuous voyage admissibility." Head taxes were designed to keep Chinese men from immigrating to Canada. Those from countries that have warm weather all year round, like countries near the equator with majority Black and brown people, were prevented from entering Canada because they were judged to be less likely to adjust to Canadian winters. People who sailed on ships that had to refuel at another port, such as ships from India, were deemed inadmissible because their voyage wasn't continuous. Canada's immigration policy used subtle language to hide its preference for English-speaking, Protestant-identifying, able-bodied, married, wealthy, and well-educated individuals who were born with a light shade of skin.

Ultimately, the dominant culture's gaze uses anti-Blackness to either superhumanize (showing Black people as exceptional) or dehumanize (showing Black people as less than human) Africans and people of African descent. An example of dehumanizing Black people is believing that they do not feel pain. This view has influenced how Black people are treated by healthcare professionals. A smallpox experiment done in the 18th century on enslaved Africans in Jamaica** and the Tuskegee syphilis experiment (1932–1972) done

---

* Prime Minister Justin Trudeau, the 23rd prime minister of Canada, is Pierre's son. Pierre died in 2000, 15 years before Justin would become leader of the nation.

** Schiebinger, Londa. *Secret Cures of Slaves: People, Plants, and Medicine in the Eighteenth-Century Atlantic World.* Stanford, CA: Stanford University Press (2017).

on African American men in the United States show a long history of medical researchers and professionals treating Black bodies as disposable. Although these experiments happened a long time ago, a study published in 2016 showed that Black patients are routinely underprescribed and undertreated for pain compared to white patients.* An example of superhumanization can be found in describing the sexuality of Black people. Black women are stereotyped as having an insatiable sexual appetite while Black men are said to be well endowed. While dehumanizing and superhumanizing Black people may seem innocuous, these stereotypes are ultimately used to create division and cause harm.

As I evaluated the data collected from patrons and workshop attendees who did anti-Blackness prompts (the prompts are also included towards the end of this chapter), the overarching theme that emerged is that Black people are dangerous. This is at the core of anti-Blackness.** A few patrons and workshop attendees wrote that they mistakenly entered bars, churches, or clubs with predominantly Black people and felt scared, awkward, or unsafe. Yet, nothing happened. They were not injured or harassed walking into the place. One patron, Arwen, wrote that after moving into a predominantly Black neighborhood, her parents visited and had the following warning:

> I moved into a part of the city where there weren't a lot of white people. I didn't know at the time that the neighborhood was being "gentrified" and I was part of that first wave. My parents never said racist things about Black people, but when they visited me for the first time, they said that this was a dangerous neighborhood. What they said made me go to businesses and stores owned by white people. When I'd walk around the neighborhood, my body would tense up whenever Black

---

* Hoffman, Kelly M., Sophie Trawalter, Jordan R. Axt, and M. Norman Oliver. "Racial Bias in Pain Assessment and Treatment Recommendations, and False Beliefs about Biological Differences between Blacks and Whites." *Psychological and Cognitive Sciences* 113, no. 16 (2016): 4296–4301. https://doi.org/10.1073/pnas.1516047113.

** If you identify as African or a person of African descent, this chapter may be difficult to read. I'm sorry I even have to write it because you'd think that the work of our intellectual ancestors, such as Marcus Garvey, Stuart Hall, bell hooks, James Baldwin, and others, would have helped us, their descendants, not to have to experience racial hate, harassment, and microaggression for yet another generation. If you identify as African or are of African descent and this chapter is feeling heavy, please care for yourself by skipping it.

people were nearby, especially Black men. As a white woman, I was nervous being around Black men who were strangers. I never had a bad experience with a Black man, but this prompt made me realize it was all part of my socialization.

This was noted in several reactions from those who did this prompt. The body tensing up, the nervous system being activated, and the heart pounding wildly were somatic responses to being near Black people. These bodily sensations happen when a human senses danger. And when encountering a Black person who they perceive as "dangerous" based on skin color alone, whether that Black person is just sitting quietly on a park bench, walking confidently along a street, or laughing jubilantly with a friend, the response is to attack, avoid, or accommodate.*

Attacking a Black person isn't necessarily about physical violence; it's also about the words used to demean and degrade. The casual use of the n-word decades after it has been made clear that this is a highly offensive and triggering word, or even lesser microaggressions, which Dictionary.com defines as "a subtle but offensive comment or action directed at a member of a marginalized group, especially a racial minority, that is often unintentionally offensive or unconsciously reinforces a stereotype,"** are ways to alienate, abuse, berate, and vilify using verbal attacks. A few patrons and workshop attendees shared experiences of using African American Vernacular English (AAVE) with their white friends in social situations to appear "cool" only to realize that doing so in a professional setting with Black people was a microaggression.

Religion is a tool used to justify anti-Blackness. I was raised in a fundamental Protestant religion and remember that the Curse of Ham*** was used to justify the enslavement of Africans and the continued mistreatment of people with darker shades of skin. One patron who was raised in the Mormon religion

---

* In his book, *The Power of a Positive No*, William Ury wrote that there are three responses someone has when hearing the word "no." I'm using these responses in this book for no other reason than to offer a different name for the three trauma responses—fight (attack), flee (avoid), and freeze/fawn (accommodate).

** Dictionary.com, s.v. "microaggression (n)," accessed November 9, 2022. https://www.dictionary.com/browse/microaggression.

*** Based on Genesis 9:20–27 in the Christian Bible when Ham saw the nakedness of his father, Noah.

shared that there was a belief that those with black skin are cursed, and those with exceedingly fair skin were delightful in the sight of God.*

When avoidance is used as a reaction to the myth of the dangerous Black person, it shows up as ignoring that skin color is an issue. One person who did this prompt said that she wasn't aware that she was even white until five years earlier. This is an example of avoidance—not recognizing the power dynamics and the unmerited advantages that come with the color of one's skin. Intellectualizing or using logic and facts to try and explain racism away is another avoidance tactic.

Citing one's shame, guilt, sensitivities, and fatigue are also ways that some avoid confronting their unconscious and conscious anti-Blackness. I was once interviewed on a podcast where I pointed out to the host that their lament over their ignorance of their unearned advantages due to being white is a form of centering.** Instead of putting the spotlight on racism and those who are harmed by it, the podcast host concentrated on explaining away their misstep and why they are not a horrible person. This, too, is a form of avoidance, where the feelings of white people take precedence over how their continued denials are hurting Black people.

One way that some accommodate is to overcompensate. They try too hard to show that they aren't racist (on Day 21, you'll explore Weaponized Kindness in more detail). This theme came up over and over as I analyzed the data from patrons. To show that they do not harbor anti-Blackness, they resort to over-the-top kindness. One patron shared that they would check on their Black friends excessively just to make sure they were okay. It was in doing the Guided Self-Reflective Activities that this patron realized they were overcompensating to cover up their uncertainty of how to act around Black people.

The myth of the dangerous Black person can cause some to treat Black children more harshly than children who have lighter shades of skin. There were a few teachers who did a prompt called The Adultification of Black Children in the Inner Field Trip Basecamp and became aware that they held Black children to a higher standard because they were taller, larger, and/or darker than their peers of the same age. One teacher, a white man, reported

---

* Based on 2 Nephi 5:21 in the Book of Mormon.

** That part of the interview was edited out of the episode that was released publicly, much to my disappointment.

that he cried after doing the prompt. He became aware that he was harsher to Black students in his class.

The function of anti-Blackness is to dehumanize people of African descent. Non-Black people who did this prompt held harmful views about Africans and people of African descent. In exchange for being The Model Minority, some non-Black racialized groups end up oppressing Black people just so they can get crumbs from the oppressor's table. A South Asian woman who attended one of my workshops shared that she feels resentment towards Black people because her experiences with racism are not included in the conversation. She acknowledged that she must keep her pain around racism to herself because she's expected to be obedient and not cause harm.

Jealousy, contempt, and resentment prevent racialized groups from coming together to fight oppression. In addition to this tension between racialized groups, there is an internalization of anti-Blackness by Africans and people of African descent. A patron who is of African Caribbean descent shared that she heard damaging messages about her coily hair and dark skin from her caregivers. As a result, she grew up hating how she looked.

Anti-Blackness causes so much division. It separates people from each other, it detaches people from themselves, and it disconnects people from creating thriving communities. The anger should be directed towards the dominant culture, one that has indoctrinated us into believing that there is nothing good about Black people. Freeing ourselves from anti-Blackness means identifying what it is, how it shows up, and naming the problem for what it is. That is a liberatory act.

What Is Possible When You Eliminate Anti-Blackness

Society becomes more innovative. There's an economic cost to anti-Blackness. One study found that racial violence due to riots, lynchings, and Jim Crow laws that took place in the United States between 1870 and 1940 prevented just over 1,000 patents from being filed.* Patents represent innovations and

---

* Cook, Lisa C. "Violence and Economic Activity: Evidence from African American Patents, 1870 to 1940." Michigan State University (2013). https://lisadcook.net/wp-content/uploads/2014/02/pats _paper17_1013_final_web.pdf.

inventions that could benefit the entire country, if not the world. So, imagine with me for a second:

- What cure could never be invented when anti-Blackness discourages a Black girl from pursuing science or math?

- What invention will never be introduced when anti-Blackness prematurely ends the life of a Black man who is no longer alive to birth a Black version of Albert Einstein?

- More practically, what business will never achieve economic prosperity when anti-Blackness prevents a Black customer with a large following on social media from dining comfortably and then writing a favorable review that brings dozens to their restaurant, gym, or store?

I understand that by reading this, it sounds like I'm equating Black people only to the labor that they can produce for a capitalist economy. What I'm trying to point out is that when Black people are free of racial discrimination and harassment, the entire population benefits economically, mentally, socially, culturally, and intellectually.

This can be extended to other racialized groups as well. For example, it has been proven that immigration is good for countries.* Yet, immigration bans and rabid policing of borders encourage pervasive beliefs that racialized groups will "harm" the country by taking jobs from "more deserving" white people. Study after study shows this to be false, and yet many are not capable of understanding that a diverse community brings diverse solutions to complex problems.

---

* A good book on this topic is *Streets of Gold: America's Untold Story of Immigrant Success* written by two economists, Ran Abramitzky and Leah Boustan. They used census data to look at the income levels of children of immigrants versus children of parents born in the United States. They found that children of immigrants were more upwardly mobile economically compared to children of parents born in the United States.

Guided Self-Reflective Activities

Step 1—Identify your mood before starting. Go to page 239 and use the Mood Tracker to capture how you're feeling.

Step 2—Black Dots (15 minutes).

	**Supplies needed:** Black marker, crayon or pen, timer.
	What to do: ✂ Set your timer to count down from 15 minutes. ✂ Draw a picture using only dots with a black marker, crayon, or pen. Do this until the timer goes off.

Use the space below to draw Black Dots.

Step 3—Journal (15 minutes).

Supplies needed: Sketchbook or journal, pen/pencil OR keyboard and screen, timer.

What to do:
- Navigate the prompt using GPS (see page 237).
- Set your timer to count down from 15 minutes.
- Capture the ramblings of your Inner Oppressor in your journal or sketchbook using the following prompts as a guide:

Prompt #1: Name a time when you judged a Black person based on nothing more than their skin color. How did your body react to their presence? What thoughts went through your mind? What words did you whisper? Who were you with? Why did you react the way you did to the presence of a Black person? How can you be more aware of this reaction?

Prompt #2: Do you have a different reaction to the Black person who is an entertainer vs. the Black person who owns a business or speaks about their ideas? If yes, why? If no, why not?

Prompt #3: Look at these phrases:
- "She is such a strong Black woman."
- "I don't see race; I see the human race."
- "I don't see color."

Although positive on the surface, how do these phrases contribute to anti-Blackness?

Step 4—Track your mood after completing the Guided Self-Reflective Activities. Go to page 239 and use the Mood Tracker to capture how you're feeling now that you're done.

Congratulations!

You have completed today's actions. Please resist the urge to move quickly to the next day's actions. If you have capacity, you can also file your Summary Report at https://summary.innerfieldtrip.com (optional). Otherwise, go to page 243 and color in the day that you completed on the Journey Tracker page, put the Inner Field Trip aside, get on with your day, then resume tomorrow at the time you booked to meet with your Inner Oppressor.

Explore Urgency

How would you react if there was a zombie apocalypse? If, suddenly, people started turning into zombies as you were waiting in line at the grocery store, picking up your child from school, or sitting on a patio with friends, how would you react? How would you operate each day and each week the zombie apocalypse continued?

The scenario above is obviously a work of fiction. Yet, real life may sometimes feel like a scene out of *The Walking Dead* or *The Last of Us,* where people are mindlessly moving from one form of stress and danger to the next. People of Historically Undesired Groups (HUGs) feel as if they go through a series of micro-crises every day when they interact with the dominant culture. Politicians, celebrities, and other famous people fill the news cycle with their never-ending messes and missteps. Social media gives us a steady stream of drama and conflict. Perhaps there's someone in your social circle who is the poster child of chaos. It seems like everything requires us to act quickly; otherwise we'll miss out.

That's what the dominant culture wants—it wants you to rush, expend a lot of energy in a short period of time, and then be too exhausted to create, innovate, and generate new ways of dismantling structural barriers. Such was the case during the Great Racial Awakening that happened after George Floyd's murder in the spring of 2020. His death created unprecedented awareness and support for the continued fight for the civil and human rights of people of African descent. While Floyd isn't the first African American to die during an encounter with law enforcement, his death was seen by millions of people around the world who had nothing else to focus on while sheltering in place due to the global pandemic.

As I shared in the introduction, many rushed into action. Witnessing such a horrible death on video with nowhere else to direct one's attention was traumatic and horrifying. For some, the only relief was to do something—anything. People rushed to put together lists of anti-racist educators to follow. People bought the books, watched the documentaries, and attended the marches. They donated money and signed up for courses. Some of my colleagues who facilitate Diversity, Equity, and Inclusion training said that they received so many inquiries, they stopped answering emails or told prospects they wouldn't be available until the following year. Some of my contemporaries saw their followers on Instagram triple and quadruple in a few short days.

On the one hand, it is a good sign that so many, no matter their race or ethnicity, felt the need to rise up against the brutal police murder of a Black man. We can take this as a sign that some progress is being made. On the other hand, we still need to examine why, in the wake of so much activism, the vast majority of those involved in protests and activism, even if they continue to hold the same ideals, have retreated to whatever they were doing before Floyd's murder.

This goes back to something we discussed at the beginning of this book: the fact that urgency and rushing keep you focused on the here and now, believing that the future is too far away and the past must be forgotten. As I shared in the introduction, too, rushing also forces you to believe that you are alone in this effort, even as you may see hundreds of thousands of people across the globe protesting. Rugged individualism trains you to believe that only you have the answers and only you have what it takes to solve the massive problem of systemic oppression. This encourages you to do more than you're emotionally, physically, financially, or mentally able to do. Then, exhausted, you retreat to the status quo and keep the machine of oppression cranking away, even as it appears most people on the ground would like things to change. The illusion of urgency is a key part of the thinking that ultimately causes vital activism to sometimes become a "trend" that quickly recedes, even when the goals of the movement are nowhere near being met.

Yes, there are some situations that require you to act with urgency. An emergency related to a natural disaster or an accident are situations where sitting back to reflect, journal, and do art is ill-advised. Emergencies require you to act fast because it's a matter of your survival, or the survival of someone in your immediate vicinity where you actually *do* have the power to impact the situation by taking acting.

But structural barriers cannot be changed overnight through urgency and individualism. It took generations for systemic oppression to take root; it'll take more than one march, workshop, or book to dismantle it. While this was discussed in the introduction, you have now met your Inner Oppressor and taken some time to focus on structural and institutional oppression, and you likely have a new understanding of it compared to when you first opened this book. You may have initially found this kind of commentary about urgency discouraging, as though what you were reading was that systemic oppression is a problem that's too big and massive to tackle, which can leave you feeling as if you shouldn't bother at all.

At this point in the quest, you may be understanding the situation differently. You may understand better that while it is good to show up at a protest, you cannot organize all of your efforts around one tragedy by yourself and expect to change the world within a month or two. Yes, you still need to pay attention to current events and crimes against HUGs, but you need to create a more sustainable approach. And to that end, this is a good time to apply such principles across your life. For example, you may want to rush through the 30-day Inner Field Trip quest now that you are already so far along. You may try to do two or three days in one sitting due to excitement or not wanting to fall behind. Jennifer, a patron, shared this after being reminded not to rush through the Inner Field Trip:

> What's the point of all the change we want in society if not so we can all actually enjoy living our lives? I think that if I sacrifice myself well enough, it will decrease the suffering of others, when in fact I am just one person and my martyrdom won't solve the world's ills. I think love and joy are much more powerful influencers than guilt and sacrifice, and I want to celebrate and encourage pleasure in myself and others.

Another patron shared that she felt guilty about missing a day or more when doing the 30-day Inner Field Trip quest. If you're still wrestling with your Inner Oppressor around perfection, go back to Day 9 and do the Guided Self-Reflective Activities again. The Inner Field Trip isn't based on an either/or paradigm. It's not "Either you do the quest on consecutive days without a miss, or you put this book on your shelf and call yourself a failure." Instead, the Inner Field Tip is both/and. You can both feel the urgency of fighting against systems of oppression and slow down enough to take one small action each day.

Sadly, just as people rushed to do something after George Floyd's death, once the intensity of the emotions died down, so, too, did people's enthusiasm to dismantle structural oppression. Some who joined my Inner Field Trip community apologetically sent messages less than a month after joining, stating that they are ending their membership due to sheer exhaustion. As a Black woman, I wish I could exit the fight for social justice and civil rights due to fatigue. Yes, it is a choice to spend much of my life engaged in the fight, but if I threw up my hands and decided not to work on Inner Field Trips or any other form of social justice work or activism, I would still face the same exact oppression as a member of a HUG. I could not return to the illusory "status quo" that only those who have considerable advantages can retreat to. It is a privilege of those in Historically Desired Groups (HDGs) to be able to pop in and out of the fight for social justice and forget about issues of oppression entirely unless they make the choice to focus on them. Most of us—given that members of HUGs comprise the majority of the world's population—do not have that luxury.

You have now reached a point in the quest where you can consider approaching things a different way. Rushing and hurrying to fix systemic oppression not only demoralizes and exhausts you, but it also causes you to miss out on acknowledging the ways that the dominant culture has calcified in your mind, body, cells, nervous system, and bones. You can use your words to convince yourself that you no longer believe and you can perform the actions that show that you no longer align with the beliefs of the dominant culture, but your body does not lie. If you identify with an HDG and you suddenly become aware of how your advantages oppress others, the next action is to sit still and feel the awareness in your body instead of discharging that chaotic energy for all to see, performing until you wear yourself out, retreat and disappear, and no lasting change has been affected.

At its core, all this rapid activity only helps you to avoid interrogating your Inner Oppressor around how systems of domination and control still live within you. Rushing to solve social injustices with intense, all-consuming, frenzied action is another way that you're using the tools of domination to dominate others. Can't see the connection? Let's go back to these lists that people create on social media. You may have noticed them circulating after an event that prompts people to quickly find someone who can help them make sense of what they witnessed. This is a good thing. However, these lists often include individuals who do not consider themselves to be social justice activists or have no recognized history in that arena. A transgender woman who is a fitness trainer may be a wonderful person to support, but that does not necessarily make her a transgender rights activist. An East Asian therapist may not be the right person to add to your #StopAsianHate list of experts if he is a family therapist with no training or even awareness of race-based PTSD. During Black History Month, employees who are Black are frequently invited by their Human Resources departments to sit on a panel called "Being Black at [insert company name]." In all cases, the person from a HUG was targeted simply due to one or more of their social, ethnic, biological, and behavioral identities (SEBBIs for short). Targeting someone, no matter your intentions, is an example of identity-based oppression.

Again, it is good to support businesses operated by HUGs, but not every member of a HUG is an activist or expert in dismantling oppression just because of their SEBBIs. The best example of this, of course, is the way that women make up a majority of the human population, yet most of us understand that we cannot just randomly and indiscriminately list every woman who has attained a remote position of prominence as an expert in feminism, gender-based violence, recovery from sexual assault, or advocating reproductive freedom. In fact, we know that most women have had little to no training in these issues, and that many women, for reasons of religious dogma, lack of freedom, or skin color advantages, do not align with these causes. If we all did, the goals of intersectional feminism would already have been attained. While being a member of a HUG does guarantee that you have faced some form of oppression in your life, it does not at all guarantee that you are an expert at dismantling that oppression, much less in helping others to do the same.

When you move fast, you tend to break things. You either injure yourself or harm others when moving at great speed. On the contrary, you do not lose anything by slowing down. As I mentioned before, a genuine emergency is one of those few times when you need to act quickly because *your individual actions* genuinely impact the outcome of the emergency. If your house is on fire and you don't call 911, journaling your feelings will not summon the firefighters to arrive and extinguish the blaze. Alternatively, the unraveling of systemic oppression is a multigenerational effort that will take millions of people all committing to some level of a lifetime of work. The work you start in your lifetime can be a gift that you pass on to your children who then pass that on to their children. Learning the art of slowing down can aid you in passing on healing rather than pain. As one popular saying goes, "If it has always run in the family, it runs out with you."*

One way that you can practice slowing down is to ground yourself in the things that bring you calm and comfort. If you're truly interested in not causing harm to others, especially those from HUGs, then pausing is one way to help your mind, body, and energy be in alignment. It is also important in our product-oriented, capitalist culture to remember that whether we are members of an HDG or a HUG, causing harm to ourselves is very rarely the best way to approach activism. By harm, I don't mean emotional discomfort, which is inevitable when meeting your Inner Oppressor. I'm referring to the loss of sleep, neglect of self-care, and burning yourself out until you feel numb. While there are famous cases of those who brought about change through martyrdom, overall, especially among those of us who are "ordinary people" and not famous or high profile, martyrdom only results in burnout and a return to the status quo. It certainly does not help anyone else in our present world or in the future.

Self-care is important when embarking on ancestor-changing work. "Grounding" is a word that refers to the techniques you would use to self-soothe when you're feeling stressed, overwhelmed, or overstimulated. Rushing can activate your nervous system and cause you to make poor decisions. Grounding, on the other hand, can help you to settle your thoughts and calm your heightened emotions so you can make better decisions. "Create a Soothie"** is a fun way to remind yourself of what you need when you're feeling anxious. Patrons shared their Soothies, and you can see in the example on the following page how one patron, Logan, slows down by taking naps, doodling, moving their body, and singing.

Other patrons and workshop attendees add cuddly blankets, dancing, watching easy television, writing, playing video games, streaming comedy shows, painting, exercising, and secondhand shopping to their Soothies. These

* Please do not attribute this quote to me. It is not mine. I have looked earnestly for the originator of this quote and have been unable to determine who originally said it. One way to know that someone did not originate a quote is when it is attributed to multiple people. That is the case with this powerful quote.

** "Create a Soothie" is adapted from Susan I. Buchalther's "Cope Cakes" in her book *250 Brief, Creative & Practical Art Therapy Techniques: A Guide for Clinicians and Clients* (2017).

are the activities and items they rely on to bring them calm and peace during frantic times.

What Is Possible When You Release the Need to Rush

Creativity is ignited. Slowing down in a nonemergent situation can help you activate your imagination. Systems of oppression need unique solutions to a multigenerational problem. When you can slow down, you are more likely to find the free time needed to develop innovative solutions.

Sustained action is prioritized over sudden movements. You understand that the work to eliminate systemic oppression is urgent, and you are also aware that you need to approach the work in small steps. People of HUGs need those from HDGs to stick with the effort for decades, not days, and that can only happen when you hurry up and slow down.

Guided Self-Reflective Activities

Step 1—Identify your mood before starting. Go to page 239 and use the Mood Tracker to capture how you're feeling.

Step 2—Create a Soothie (15 minutes).

<table>
<tr>
<td rowspan="2"></td>
<td>Supplies needed: Colored markers, pens, pastels, paints or crayons, timer.</td>
</tr>
<tr>
<td>

What to do:
- Set your timer to count down from 15 minutes.
- Draw an outline of a tall drinking glass. Then, fill it with words representing the activities, people, places, or items that you can rely on to provide calm. Decorate your Soothie if you have time.
- Stop once the timer goes off.

</td>
</tr>
</table>

Use the space below to create a Soothie.

Step 3—Journal (15 minutes).

Supplies needed: Sketchbook or journal, pen/pencil OR keyboard and screen, timer.

What to do:

- Navigate the prompt using GPS (see page 237).
- Set your timer to count down from 15 minutes.
- Capture the ramblings of your Inner Oppressor in your journal or sketchbook using the following prompts as a guide:

Prompt #1: Where in your body do you feel resistance to slowing down? Point to that area of your body where a sensation is coming up. What is your Inner Oppressor trying to reveal to you?

Prompt #2: Who or what do you need to release to make room for what shows up in your Soothie? How can you make what's in your Soothie part of your day-to-day activities?

Step 4—Track your mood after completing the Guided Self-Reflective Activities. Go to page 239 and use the Mood Tracker to capture how you're feeling now that you're done.

Congratulations!

You have completed today's actions. Please resist the urge to move quickly to the next day's actions. If you have capacity, you can also file your Summary Report at https://summary.innerfieldtrip.com (optional). Otherwise, go to page 243 and color in the day that you completed on the Journey Tracker page, put the Inner Field Trip aside, get on with your day, then resume tomorrow at the time you booked to meet with your Inner Oppressor.

Explore Harshness

I love hiking in the winter. Although I hike in any season, winter hiking brings a particular happiness. Hearing my boots crunching in the snow and ice, seeing nothing but a gray-and-white palette on the horizon, and hearing but a few errant chirps and slight rustles in the bushes as the ground critters move about is a reminder that while winter makes nature appear dead, life still stirs. Despite my fondness for being outside in the winter, there have been a few times when I've had to turn around and venture back to my car due to the cold, billowing wind. A wintry wind brings a particular harshness to the season that can challenge even the most winter-sturdy Canadian.

I expect winter's chilly wind to be harsh; I don't expect the same from people. Yet, human beings can also be coarse and unfeeling, especially when dealing with those whose suffering makes them uncomfortable. It seems that there's a special type of harshness reserved for those who are helpless, defenseless, or unprotected. Migrants fleeing unimaginable cruelty in their country of origin are left to languish in prisons and refugee tent encampments in countries they believe can provide safety. Victims of violence are subjected to unrelenting scrutiny over their choice to be where they have every right to be, what they were wearing, or how they "should" have defended themselves. People who are homeless are told to work harder to find stable housing and stop seeking handouts. Veterans suffering from post-traumatic stress lose government funding to life-enhancing mental health services, even as the public is told to respect our troops. Women who are involuntarily child-free are berated unmercifully about not trying hard enough to conceive. These situations should elicit empathy, concern, and care; instead, they too often activate scorn, mockery, and disdain.

The dominant culture teaches us that life is tough. "No one gets a free ticket," some utter as they justify a harsh life using a tired cliché. We are socialized to believe that the antidote to a harsh life is to stay mentally positive and somehow just "overcome" adversity. Having a "stiff upper lip" is another trite cliché that's uttered when a person displays fortitude and self-restraint in the face of adversity. This toxic positivity has only led us to repress and hide our natural emotions for fear of judgment. This is the frustrating contradiction within the dominant culture's playbook. Life is harsh, says the dominant culture, but if something bad happens to you, it's your own fault. You did not think positively enough, or your faith in your Creator was not strong enough, or you put yourself in the wrong place at the wrong time, the nattering nabobs of negativity* utter. Knowing that this is the reaction that victims and sufferers receive, your Inner Oppressor compels you to stay silent when something bad happens to you. Your Inner Oppressor has learned to abide by the rules of the dominant culture to keep you safe, secure, and supported.

You may believe that you do act with compassion. Perhaps you're one of the first to donate funds to someone who's in a bad spot. Sometimes, you don't provide aid because, subconsciously, you don't believe the person deserves your help due to their social, ethnic, biological, or behavioral identities (SEBBIs). In other words, you will act compassionately to one group of people and not to another. After doing this prompt, some patrons and workshop attendees expressed their horror at some of the thoughts that came up through journaling. One expressed that she has a hard time believing that some Historically Undesired Groups (HUGs) are suffering because they're dancing, singing, and appear as if they're having a good life. Another stated that some HUGs own real estate and are wealthier than they are, so it appears that HUGs are doing fine. Others within Historically Desired Groups (HDGs) state that they've dealt with ailments, illnesses, and poverty and wonder who will stand for them.

Some will use their personal challenges as an excuse to act with harshness towards others. Others will use their sensitivities, intuition, or empathy as an excuse to disengage from the work of challenging the traits of the dominant culture within themselves, saying that the work is "too upsetting" and that it is an act of self-care to avoid negative news and exhausting activism work. As a mental wellness advocate, I'm all for people prioritizing their self-care. There

---

* Former vice president of the United States Spiro Agnew called those who criticized then president Richard Nixon "nattering nabobs of negativity."

are some, however, who weaponize their mental health condition to use as a tool to suppress, silence, and shut down conversations around identity-based oppression.*

Often, what this leads to is a prioritization of whose suffering is more worthy of compassion. Some believe that people from HDGs are more deserving of empathy than those from HUGs. For some, seeing people from HUGs in any capacity except in a state of suffering invokes feelings of harshness. The dominant culture conditions us to believe that if HUGs aren't walking around with long faces, slumped shoulders, waxy skin, brittle hair, and dull eyes,** then it means oppression no longer exists. Seeing HUGs not in a state of suffering can invoke feelings of contempt, confusion, and bitterness. One patron who worked through this prompt, a white woman, shared how her early experience traveling the world with her missionary parents helped shape how she views Black and brown people. She explained feeling a lump forming in her throat and irritation flooding her body when seeing HUGs in their joy. She realized that being on those mission trips with her parents conditioned her into seeing Black and brown people in need of white people to save them.

For some, their compassion is time limited. They may show up for a grieving family at the funeral, but if the family is still grieving a year from now, they may respond with a roll of the eyes. One patron shared that his Inner Oppressor revealed his disdain for those who are grieving. He recalled attending the funeral with a friend whose mom died unexpectedly. He was very supportive of his friend at the funeral. Two years later, his friend was still grieving, and the patron reacted by telling his friend to move on. He could see the connection between how he reacted to his friend and how he responds to those facing identity-based oppression.

In some cases, harshness was used by parents to keep their children safe. This is especially true in some immigrant families. Being harsh was an attempt by some immigrant parents to help their children behave so that they would

---

* I want to make *very* clear that mental health disorders are complex. There are multiple factors that cause mental illness. If someone needs to disengage to protect their mental wellness, I support that decision. Likewise, someone acting in an inhumane, oppressive, or evil way is not an automatic sign of mental illness, and most violent offenders are not "mentally ill" per se. We need to stop associating mass shootings, terrorist acts, and criminality with mental illness. It's ableist, cruel, and unethical.

** This description was inspired by a scene from the sitcom *Frasier*, in an episode called "The Innkeepers," where one of the characters, Niles, compares the decline of a five-star restaurant to that of a Hollywood actor one worshiped as a child who has aged ungracefully.

be accepted by the dominant culture. Countless patrons and workshop attendees shared their early experience with immigrant parents who would act in a cold and unfeeling way to their frustrations and complaints. Although many realized that being stern and tough was their parents' way of protecting them, it didn't make their harshness any easier to accept.

Some would say that a firm hand is needed to raise children. There is, however, a difference between being firm and being harsh. Being firm means that you stick to your principles. If young Johnny asks for a chocolate bar for the umpteenth time even though you told him that dinner will soon be served, then telling Johnny no for the umpteenth time is an act of being firm. However, if you tell Johnny that he's going to get fat and all the kids at school will make fun of him to discourage him from asking for chocolate again, then this is an example of harsh and shaming behavior.

Some women of color use harshness to protect themselves from the damaging effects of racism and sexism. They may behave coldly to their loved ones, such as their children, in a conscious or unconscious attempt to prepare them for the harsh world. People of African descent who did this prompt reported that their parents, caregivers, and extended family members taught them to hide their feelings. One patron remembered the coldness that her paternal grandmother expressed, never expressing love verbally or physically. Another shared that by being stoic, she would protect herself from feeling the sting of the intersection of racism and sexism.

As a hiker, I can replace the harshness of a blustering, chilly winter wind with the warmth of the hot air blowing through the vents after returning to my car. You can replace the coarseness that you've shown yourself or others with gentleness, softness, and warmth. If you're not used to being treated in a soft and gentle way, surrounding yourself with softness and gentleness is one way to get used to a new way of being. To treat others with gentleness, you first need to develop a softness habit. Uttering kind words to yourself is a start (see Day 21 on Weaponized Kindness). In this prompt, allowing soft and fuzzy things to touch your skin and surround your body is one way to develop a gentle state of mind.

When some hear harshness and then its opposite, softness, they think of a masculine-feminine paradigm. Not only is this model exclusionary, but it also gives the impression that only people who identify as women can be soft and gentle—or require softness or gentleness. Gentleness is needed by *all* genders because it's about extending tenderness, and not blame, ridicule, or impatience, to those who are suffering. Gentleness is an antidote to shame. An older workshop attendee lamented about the relationship he does not have with his adult sons. While doing this prompt, he realized that he showed his sons nothing but harshness, such as telling them to "Suck it up" or "Stop acting like a girl" whenever they cried. He wondered how different his relationship with his sons would be if he had only shown them some kindness. He ended by saying, "Maybe they'll forgive me."

What Is Possible When You Release Harshness

Community care grows. Instead of only being compassionate towards certain people and for a certain period, you extend compassion due to shared humanity. Community care can only happen, however, if you understand how to care for yourself. It is far easier to be gentle and soft towards others when you are familiar with how it feels.

Guided Self-Reflective Activities

Step 1—Identify your mood before starting. Go to page 239 and use the Mood Tracker to capture how you're feeling.

Step 2—Comfy Fort (15 minutes).

<table>
<tr>
<td rowspan="2"></td>
<td>Supplies needed: Pillows, blankets, comforters, and sheets PLUS crayons, paints, markers or colored pens.</td>
</tr>
<tr>
<td>

What to do:

- Build your fort under your desk, on a sofa, on a bed, in the closet, or any other spot where you can sit comfortably using the soft items that you gathered.
- (OPTIONAL) If you'd like to hold or cuddle something soft in your hands or arms, a teddy bear, scarf, pet, or a throw blanket are options. Make sure they are soft.
- Set your timer to count down from 15 minutes.
- Doodle one word or phrase describing what you're feeling while being under the fort.

</td>
</tr>
</table>

Use the space below to doodle one word or phrase that describes how you feel as you sit under your Comfy Fort.

Step 3—Journal (15 minutes).

Supplies needed: Sketchbook or journal, pen/pencil OR keyboard and screen, timer.

What to do:

- Navigate the prompt using GPS (see page 237).
- Set your timer to count down from 15 minutes.
- Capture the ramblings of your Inner Oppressor in your journal or sketchbook using the following prompts as a guide:

Prompt #1: What does the word or phrase that you doodled on the previous page tell you about your reaction to softness and coziness?

Prompt #2: In what ways can you add more softness, coziness, and cushiness to your day-to-day life? Is this something you even want to do? Why or why not?

Prompt #3: What unhelpful beliefs do you hold, causing you to misinterpret someone's suffering? How can this line of thinking prevent you from seeing their strengths? How can it prevent you from extending grace?

Step 4—Track your mood after completing the Guided Self-Reflective Activities. Go to page 239 and use the Mood Tracker to capture how you're feeling now that you're done.

Congratulations!

You have completed today's actions. Please resist the urge to move quickly to the next day's actions. If you have capacity, you can also file your Summary Report at https://summary.innerfieldtrip.com (optional). Otherwise, go to page 243 and color in the day that you completed on the Journey Tracker page, put the Inner Field Trip aside, get on with your day, then resume tomorrow at the time you booked to meet with your Inner Oppressor.

Active Rest Stop

Once again, you have reached another Active Rest Stop. They are built into the 30-day Inner Field Trip quest so you can take a moment to pause. You encountered one on Day 11, another one today, and there will be two more, on Days 20 and 25. To remind yourself why we take a moment to pause during the Inner Field Trip, go back and review Day 11.

What to Do During an Active Rest Stop

As a reminder, instead of reviewing the art or writings you produced during the previous three or four days, you will instead focus on creating, building, composing, moving, or making. Resmaa Menakem recommends discharging and dispersing energy nurtured through conflict or high-stress situations by using movement, such as dance, playing sports, exercise, or physical labor.[*] Movement is encouraged during the Active Rest Stop, and so, too, are creative and artistic pursuits. The infographic on the following page gives some ideas on what you can do during the Active Rest Stop.

The font may be a bit small, so I've listed the six categories and related activities below:

- **Build It**—Building Blocks, Popsicle Sticks, Toothpicks, Glue Gun, Model Toy, Jigsaw Puzzle, Slime, Play-Doh, Mimetic Sand

- **Make It**—Knitting, Sewing, Crocheting, Needlepoint, Embroidery, Beading, Woodworking, Baking

---

* Menakem, Resmaa. *My Grandmother's Hands: Racialized Trauma and the Pathway to Mending Our Hearts and Bodies*. Las Vegas: Central Recovery Press (2017): Chapter 12.

- **Illustrate It**—Painting, Drawing, Cartooning, Collaging, Junk Journaling, Diamond Painting, Lettering

- **Compose/Write It**—Music, Screenplay, Memoir, Pandemic Reflections, Creative Writing, TV Script, One-Person Show, Play, Poetry

- **Move It**—Walking, Hiking, Dancing, Cycling, Trampolining, Skating, Exercising

- **Reflect on It**—Meditating, Praying, Napping, Deep Breathing, Listening to Calm Music, Yoga, Bubble Bathing, Playing Calm Music on an Instrument

Some things to remember when engaging in an Active Rest Stop:

- You're not doing this to be seen, published, or applauded. In other words, let go of any expectation of what your creation could become. Just be in the creating mood.

✂ It's best to do the activity solo, but if you want to include someone, choose someone with the most childlike personality. You don't want to do this with someone who's going to descend into criticism or complaints (whether directed at you or themselves).

✂ The activity you choose for the Active Rest Stop can be the same one you do during the next one, or totally different.

✂ Set the timer for 30 minutes and then let your creativity take over. Color outside the lines. Leave the mess on the floor. Play a wrong note. Write using run-on sentences. Use your nondominant hand to paint. Create a Play-Doh tree with red bark and purple leaves. Enjoy the messiness of the activity and release perfection.

Active Rest Stop Activities

Step 1—Identify your mood before starting. Go to page 239 and use the Mood Tracker Ring to capture how you're feeling.

Step 2—Engage in the Active Rest Stop (30 minutes).

	**Supplies needed:** Materials to engage in the Active Rest Stop, timer.
	What to do: ✂ Choose one Active Rest Stop activity. ✂ Take a few minutes to set up your play or studio space. ✂ Start the timer, then engage in the activity until the timer goes off.

Step 3—Fill in the blanks. Once the timer goes off and before tidying up your play or studio space, complete the sentences below. Spend no more than 15 seconds on each question and jot down some thoughts.

After engaging in the Active Rest Stop, my Inner Oppressor revealed:

_____

_____

_____

_____

It's no wonder because:

_____

_____

_____

_____

Therefore, the one action I will take is:

_____

_____

_____

_____

Step 4—Track your mood after completing the Guided Self-Reflective Activities. Go to page 239 and use the Mood Tracker Ring to capture how you're feeling now that you're done.

Congratulations!

You have completed today's actions. Please resist the urge to move quickly to the next day's actions. If you have capacity, you can also file your Summary Report at https://summary.innerfieldtrip.com (optional). Otherwise, go to page 243 and color in the day that you completed on the Journey Tracker page, put the Inner Field Trip aside, get on with your day, then resume tomorrow at the time you booked to meet with your Inner Oppressor.

Explore Body Insecurity

I'm a fan of *RuPaul's Drag Race*. I instantly fell in love with the artistry and pageantry of this reality competition show after watching the first season in 2009. Since then, the show has expanded to include competition shows in different countries, such as Canada, Britain, Australia, New Zealand, Belgium, Thailand, Spain, and the Philippines, as well as all-star editions where the most popular or controversial drag queens from previous episodes are welcomed back to compete.

Although the clothing and makeup are a wonder to behold, I'm equally inspired by the stories told by the contestants as they adorn themselves. Body image and mental health challenges are the most heartbreaking to hear. Some share that they were rejected by those close to them due to the size and color of their bodies or how they choose to express their gender identity. Performing in drag is often the only place they've ever felt that their bodies were accepted.

We live in a culture where people believe that they can say anything about other people's bodies. Bodies are critiqued by family members, scorned by strangers, and judged by bystanders. These critiques take place in person, through mainstream media, or online. Body insecurity is defined as a lack of confidence around the physical structure or features of one's body. Having a temporary concern for an area of your body is natural, but outright animosity is a problem.* When that resentment is nurtured by the dominant culture, with

---

* Having a temporary dislike for an area of one's body differs from body dysmorphic disorder (BDD), which is characterized by preoccupation with "one or more perceived defects or flaws in their physical

its rules on what type of body is deemed desirable, it can disconnect you from your body. We then spend our time, as Sonya Renee Taylor writes in her book *The Body Is Not an Apology*, constantly apologizing for our bodies because we believe our bodies are wrong. The more we apologize for the size, color, gender identity, and age of our bodies, the more we confirm a system that demands others apologize for theirs as well. As Taylor shares, "We have ranked our bodies against the bodies of others, deciding they are greater or lesser than our own based on the prejudices and biases we inherited."[*]

Historically Desired Groups (HDGs) have the traits that are deemed preferable by the dominant culture and don't have a lot of apologizing to do.[**] Those desirable traits, as listed on Day 1, are light shade of skin, able body, neurotypical, young-looking, tall, mentally and physically healthy (disease-free or addiction-free), smooth and light-colored hair (but not gray), few to no freckles, perfect or normal eyesight, narrow nose, right-handed, and thin lips. There are also gender-specific traits desired by the dominant culture. For people who identify as women, long, flowing hair and a thin or slim build are desired in addition to having fuller, "pouty" lips,[***] while in people who identify as men, being athletic and muscular are preferred in addition to the list of traits already mentioned.

Some men within Historically Undesired Groups (HUGs) will never meet the dominant culture's standards of masculinity. One patron, an East Asian man, lamented about comments he's received being a short and skinny man. He

appearance," according to the *Diagnostic & Statistical Manual of Mental Disorders*, 5th edition. BDD can coexist with other mental health conditions, such as eating disorders, obsessive-compulsive disorder, depression, and social anxiety disorder. When the preoccupation with one's body interferes with day-to-day functioning, such as missing school or work or avoiding social situations, the person needs to consult their primary care physician for a referral to a psychologist or psychiatrist for an official diagnosis.

* Taylor, Sonya Renee. *The Body Is Not an Apology: The Power of Radical Self-Love*. Oakland: Berrett-Koehler Publishers (2018): 13.

** While it is true that HDGs face far less institutional castigation for their bodies than HUGs, it is also notable that disordered eating was for many years most prevalent in white girls/women. Sadly, the internet and social media have now made disordered eating a more equal opportunity form of self-destruction that impacts people of all races and genders, but the fact that this prevalence was initially so high in those with skin-color privilege indicates just how widespread body shame and the feeling of being outwardly judged for our bodies is in our culture and how it is weaponized against us all.

*** This is one of the few areas in which white people have now made an industry out of looking more like Black people, as white women in particular spend untold amounts getting collagen injections into their lips, using lip-plumpers, and so on.

says that he tries to ignore it by letting his good attitude cover up what he's been socialized to believe is a shortcoming. For other HUGs, the very traits that are deemed desirable by the dominant culture can become a liability. Height is seen as a desirable trait in men; however, it is interpreted as a threat in Black men. In one study, researchers found that police in New York stopped tall Black men at a disproportionate rate compared to tall white men.* Height is also weaponized against Black children, who tend to be taller than their peers of the same age.**,*** As a result of a function of biology, Black children are seen as less innocent and in need of less nurturing, protection, support, and comfort. This is known as "adultification" and is defined as:

> [A] form of dehumanization, robbing Black children of the very essence of what makes childhood distinct from all other developmental periods: innocence. Adultification contributes to a false narrative that black youths' transgressions are intentional and malicious, instead of the result of immature decision making—a key characteristic of childhood.****

For some who belong to HUGs, their curvy bodies have been hypersexualized in utterly uninvited ways by the dominant culture. Big butts, thick thighs, and large bosoms are natural for many women due to genetics, especially those who identify as Black or Latina. Having curvy attributes should not be a "trend," nor are those physical traits an implicit invitation to be talked about, stared at, or discussed. Having a curvy body is not synonymous with giving others a license to make assumptions about the curvy person's sexual preferences or sexuality, or to hypersexualize them just because of the shape their body has naturally taken. The shape of someone's body is not in any way an

* Hester, Neil, and Kurt Gray. "For Black men, Being Tall Increases Threat Stereotyping and Police Stops," *PNAS* 115, No. 11 (February 2018): 2711–2715. https://doi.org/10.1073/pnas.1714454115.

** Hancock, Caroline, Silvana Bettiol, and Lesley Smith. "Socioeconomic Variation in Height: Analysis of National Child Measurement Programme Data for England." *Archives of Disease in Childhood* 101, No. 5 (January 2016): 413–414. http://dx.doi.org/10.1136/archdischild-2015-308431.

*** Komlos, John, and Arian Breitfelder. "Differences in the Physical Growth of US-born Black and White Children and Adolescents Ages 2–19, Born 1942–2002." *Annals of Human Biology* 35, No. 1 (January/February 2008): 11–21. https://doi.org/10.1080/03014460701747176.

**** Epstein, Rebecca, Jamilia J. Blake, and Thalia Gonzalez. *Girlhood Interrupted: The Erasure of Black Girls' Childhood.* Washington, DC: Georgetown Law Center on Poverty and Inequality (2017). https://genderjusticeandopportunity.georgetown.edu/wp-content/uploads/2020/06/girlhood-interrupted.pdf.

indicator of their libido, nor is having a higher libido (for people of any gender or size) an indication of wanting predatory attention from strangers, colleagues, and so on.

Having to apologize for, change, and amplify certain characteristics to hide a perceived physical shortcoming to make your body conform to the dominant culture's standards can be exhausting. Individuals from HUGs buy products or invest in costly image altering procedures to fit in. For example, in countries where most of the population has brown skin, like in India or the Caribbean, whitening creams are used to lighten the pigmentation in their skin. In a show called *Indian Matchmaking*, those seeking dates with the help of a matchmaker often ask to be paired with someone who is educated, competent, and not too dark.*

This preference for people with a lighter shade of skin is what's known as "colorism" or "shadism." The preference for paler skin in cultures where there are few white people is a symptom of centuries of colonization. Beauty standards based on European ideals have become toxically pervasive even in countries where most of the population is made up of non-European people. In South Korea, many people attempt to achieve a "crease" in the eyelid or more prominent bridge on the nose, physical characteristics more common among people of European descent.

Aging is another issue that can cause body insecurity. The dominant culture is obsessed with youthfulness. It contends that youthfulness is vital, positive, and exciting. Being young—and doing whatever you can to look young—is held up as the ideal. There are arguments that assert that youthfulness is a biological preference due to the necessity of furthering the species through having children. From an evolutionary standpoint, there is a tendency for some to favor those who are still "of childbearing age." However, as more people have children later in life, the biological arguments are insufficient to explain the continued preference for youthfulness.

The extreme bias against and desexualization of middle-aged and older people causes some to minimize the signs of aging. There are endless commercials and social media ads encouraging one to cover up those gray hairs using dyes, get rid of wrinkles using creams, and turn back the signs of aging

---

* Pathak, Sushmita. "Netflix's 'Indian Matchmaking' Is the Talk of India—And Not in a Good Way." NPR, June 26, 2020. https://www.npr.org/sections/goatsandsoda/2020/07/26/895008997/netflixs -indian-matchmaking-is-the-talk-of-india-and-not-in-a-good-way.

using surgical interventions. Older people, especially those who present themselves as women, are hardly shown in television shows, films, or ads. If they are featured, they are the butt of endless jokes. While those who identify as men do fare better than women in this regard, if a man is not a movie star or celebrity, he, too, is likely to begin feeling invisible by his fifties. Older people face difficulties finding work or ascending in the workplace, often being passed over for younger candidates who have less experience. As a result, some are afraid of growing older. Capitalism diminishes the role of elders because their labor can no longer be extracted.

What is said about our bodies can create wounds, and what our bodies are put through can create trauma. The wounds and trauma, left unaddressed, disconnect us from our bodies. In his book *The Body Keep Score*, Dr. Bessel van der Kolk states that trauma causes certain areas of the brain to shut down. When that happens, the body sensations associated with that area of the brain are no longer felt:

> The price for ignoring or distorting the body's messages is being unable to detect what is truly dangerous or harmful for you and, just as bad, what is safe or nourishing. Self-regulation depends on having a friendly relationship with your body. Without it you have to rely on external regulation—from medication, drugs like alcohol, constant reassurance, or compulsive compliance with the wishes of others.*

Staying in your head and ignoring your body causes you to intellectualize every experience. Intellectualization of identity-based oppression, the process of thinking about or discussing a subject using facts and data without involving your emotions or feelings, is a defense mechanism used by your Inner Oppressor to prioritize your safety and security. Intellectualization is how you rationalize identity-based oppression as being an out-of-body experience.

Any abuse, violence, or harassment against your body leaves an imprint. This experience causes you to reject aspects of your body. The trauma isn't just physical; it also includes verbal assaults. The messages you received about the size, color, or appearance of your body take a toll. It doesn't help that the dominant culture creates narratives through books, television shows,

---

* van der Kolk, Bessel. *The Body Keeps Score: Brain, Mind, and Body in the Healing of Trauma*. New York: Penguin Group (2014): 120.

magazines, songs, and other pop-culture tools to push the message that some bodies are wrong based on physical characteristics that cannot be changed.

The beauty and body standards created by the dominant culture have become increasingly impossible to reach for both HUGs and HDGs. No one in real life can remain eighteen forever or walk around airbrushed and technically altered to appear "perfect" as is often the case in media, from fashion magazines to Instagram. Although HDGs do not face the same levels of societal disapproval for their bodies as do HUGs, body insecurity has become so pervasive in our culture that it negatively impacts almost everyone. Even celebrities feel the pressure to alter their bodies to avoid ageism, sexism, racism, and ableism. A culture has become collectively sick with regard to body image issues when even its icons of beauty are full of self-loathing, insecurity, and fear.

Body insecurity needs to be replaced by body confidence. Body confidence, an appreciation of one's physical attributes and traits, can shield you from the damaging messages expressed by the dominant culture and its foot soldiers. Being body confident doesn't mean that you will never notice a "flaw" or have complex feelings about a change in or on your body ever again. It will, however, help you to express gratitude for what your body has done and what it continues to do for you. Patrons and workshop attendees who chose to write a letter to their bodies expressed a newfound appreciation for what their bodies have done for them. They identified bitterness, judgment, and internalized fatphobia and decided to have a better relationship with their bodies. Those who noticed deeper issues made a commitment to work with a therapist.

What Is Possible When You Release Body Insecurity

Both/and is possible. Your body holds memories, both good and bad. You can hold information about the wounds your body has suffered and also make room for the wisdom your body has to tell you. You can understand the facts *and* get in tune with your feelings. Your mind and your body can work together for your good (especially given that the mind/body dichotomy is largely false anyway). Knowing that this dynamic exists makes you more open to seeing the complexities in each unique situation.

Intuition is sharpened. Healing your body's wounds helps you get more in tune with your deepest truths. These truths are communicated to you through sensations. As Dr. van der Kolk points out, when you ignore the sensations in your body, you miss out on the cues that can inform you if something or someone is safe. Feeling confidence in your body helps to heighten your intuition, connecting you with generations of guidance. Instead of believing the stories that the dominant culture tells you about your body, you trust your intuition.

Guided Self-Reflective Activities

Step 1—Identify your mood before starting. Go to page 239 and use the Mood Tracker to capture how you're feeling.

Step 2—Body Part Gratitude (15 minutes).

Supplies needed: Colored markers or pens, timer.
What to do: ✂ Set your timer to count down from 15 minutes. ✂ With your writing instrument, doodle or draw the area of your body that you have the most awkward relationship with. ✂ Draw it several times, color it in, and/or use other shapes to illustrate that body part until the timer goes off.

Use the space below to doodle your body part.

Step 3—Journal (15 minutes).

Supplies needed: Sketchbook or journal, pen/pencil OR keyboard and screen, timer.

What to do:

- Navigate the prompt using GPS (see page 237).
- Set your timer to count down from 15 minutes.
- Capture the ramblings of your Inner Oppressor in your journal or sketchbook using the following prompts as a guide:

Prompt #1: What body part did you choose to recognize on the previous page? Why do you hold judgment around that part of your body? How can you heal the pain you feel around the way you view your body or body part?

Prompt #2: How do those who share your ethnicity or nationality treat the body? How have these messages informed how you view your body today? What needs to change?

Prompt #3: Write an honest letter to your body starting off with "Dear Body," then write expressively for 15 minutes. How can you use what you wrote to start having a different conversation with—and about—your body?

Step 4—Track your mood after completing the Guided Self-Reflective Activities. Go to page 239 and use the Mood Tracker to capture how you're feeling now that you're done.

Congratulations!

You have completed today's actions. Please resist the urge to move quickly to the next day's actions. If you have capacity, you can also file your Summary Report at https://summary.innerfieldtrip.com (optional). Otherwise, go to page 243 and color in the day that you completed on the Journey Tracker page, put the Inner Field Trip aside, get on with your day, then resume tomorrow at the time you booked to meet with your Inner Oppressor.

DAY SEVENTEEN

Approaching the Lookout

There are so many tales that I could tell about my hiking adventures. I've been on hikes where I got lost (yes, even with a map in hand), had the heel fall off my hiking boot two hours into the hike, and was chased by a wild turkey for about half a mile. There was one time I was nearly crushed by a large tree that fell a few meters behind me. Once, I had to go off trail to relieve myself and didn't notice that a large wasp's nest was above my head until I stood up. Sometimes, the issues are mental. There was one time when my mind convinced me that I was being followed, even though I was the only one on the trail. I was frightened by the sounds of the chipmunks and squirrels running through the bushes and dead tree trunks aligning the trail.

None of these were enough to cause me to abandon the hike. Not only is completing the hike a source of personal accomplishment, but there is often an attraction along the trail that motivates one to continue forward. A waterfall, summit, lake, or lookout* are some of the naturally occurring wonders that await the hiker midway through their journey. This natural wonder is a boost after being on the trail for a few hours.

You are now just over the halfway mark in your Inner Field Trip quest, at the proverbial lookout. Not only are you midway through the book, but you are also halfway through Part 2, the section containing the Guided Self-Reflective Activities. Each day, you've met with your Inner Oppressor to explore perfection, rugged individualism, anti-Blackness, urgency, harshness, and body

---

* A lookout is a spot along the hiking trail where you can rest and observe the view of a city, town, or valley from a point above.

insecurity. Getting this far is a cause for celebration. You have activated your Inner Oppressor using self-reflective art, captured its ramblings using self-reflective journaling, and made sense of it all using compassionate intro-spection. You've also nourished your mind, body, and soul using Active Rest Stops to add fun, pleasure, and play as part of the quest.

This is a critical point in the Inner Field Trip quest. Your Inner Oppressor may be pressuring you to stop, as it believes you've done enough. Or it may be using guilt or shame to make you feel bad about missing a few days here and there. You may feel tempted to quit the Inner Field Trip because you're exhausted. Perhaps you've noticed unfamiliar sensations in your body that occur before, during, or after meeting your Inner Oppressor. Contempt, anger, sadness, disgust, and apathy may be rising within you, and your Inner Oppressor is using those emotions to compel you to abandon the quest.

Hikers know that while the lookout is a reward for traversing the rugged trail, they still have to loop their way back to the trailhead. The trailhead is both where the hiker started their hike and where it ends after they loop back. Reaching the midway point isn't the end of the hike. If it took one to three hours to get to the lookout, it'd take just as long (if not longer) to get back to the parking lot. The journey back to the trailhead can feel extra long because the reward was already enjoyed. Standing on a hill overlooking the city, town, or valley contains a breathtaking view. The thought of hiking back to the trailhead after enjoying a respite can be a little bit discouraging.

Despite this, hikers know that the only way to complete the excursion is to return to the trailhead. Doing so means they'll get to the vehicle that will transport them back to their accommodation where they can enjoy a hot meal and hot shower. If the hiker lacks desire to leave the lookout, they can boost their mood by addressing their mindset, loading up on nutrients, and using the encouragement from others in the hiking group to raise their energy.

As you look ahead to completing the final 12 days of the Inner Field Trip quest, you'll use today, Day 17, to review the motivations you identified in Days 1–7. Recalling why you wanted to meet your Inner Oppressor to explore your unconscious biases, as well as who you hope to become after you've completed your inner quest, can help you continue this excursion in a courageous, brave, and fierce way.

Guided Self-Reflective Activities

Step 1—Identify your mood before starting. Go to page 239 and use the Mood Tracker to capture how you're feeling.

Step 2—Fill in the sections below by copying the responses from Days 1–7. How do you want to use your social, ethnic, biological, and behavioral advantages more responsibly? Review your journal writings from Day 1 and write a summary below.

_____

_____

_____

_____

What type of ancestor do you want to become so you FIRE up your legacy after going through the Inner Field Trip? Review your responses from Day 2 and write a summary below.

_____

_____

_____

_____

What day and time did you book a can't-miss meeting with your Inner Oppressor? Have you been consistent with that meeting time, or does it need to change? Review your answer on Day 3, write it down below, then decide if that meeting time needs to change.

_____

_____

_____

_____

Where did you set up your cozy grotto to meet with your Inner Oppressor? Do you have to modify that spot to help you meet your Inner Oppressor more consistently? Review your answer on Day 4, write it down below, then decide if the location of your cozy grotto needs to change.

_____

_____

_____

_____

What tools are you using to do the Guided Self-Reflective Activities? Do they need to change so you can meet your Inner Oppressor more consistently?

Review your answer on Day 5, write it down below, then decide if you need to make changes.

_____

_____

_____

_____

What did you "pack" in your Endurance Kit (EK) to deal with Journey Fatigue? Review your EK from Day 6, write a summary below, then decide if you need to make changes.

_____

_____

_____

_____

Finally, how have you treated yourself when you missed a day or two (or more)? Review your answer on Day 7, write a summary below, then decide how you'll continue to be gentle with yourself.

_____

_____

_____

_____

Step 3—Be in Community. As you review the answers above, you may determine that what you need is support from those who are journeying along this path. Although you're journeying on the Inner Field Trip by yourself, you are not alone. You can join the Inner Field Trip Basecamp (IFTB), an online community where other Brave Trekkers gather to support each other. Joining the

IFTB would be the equivalent of throwing up an emergency flare to signal that you need assistance. Visit basecamp.innerfieldtrip.com for more information.

Step 4—Track your mood after completing the Guided Self-Reflective Activities. Go to page 239 and use the Mood Tracker to capture how you're feeling now that you're done.

Congratulations!

You have completed today's actions. Please resist the urge to move quickly to the next day's actions. If you have capacity, you can also file your Summary Report at https://summary.innerfieldtrip.com (optional). Otherwise, go to page 243 and color in the day that you completed on the Journey Tracker page, put the Inner Field Trip aside, get on with your day, then resume tomorrow at the time you booked to meet with your Inner Oppressor.

Explore People Pleasing

There's an episode of *Seinfeld** where George Constanza, played by Jason Alexander, learns that Jerry's new girlfriend, Jody, doesn't like George. George spends the rest of the episode doing everything he can to get her to like him. He carries her massage table to the elevator and then flags a taxi for her even though Jody refuses his help multiple times. He then wails to his girlfriend that Jody doesn't like him. This leads to George's girlfriend breaking up with him over his obsession about not being liked. George then pursues Jody after learning that Jerry broke up with her.

George's response to Jody not liking him is an example of people pleasing, the act of putting other people's needs before your own because you only feel worthwhile if others are overtly giving their approval. When you have fuzzy, porous, or weak boundaries, other people dictate your labor, energy, and where to put your attention. You then end up giving up too much, too soon, and too often, leading to feeling trapped, tense, and tired.

Capitalism, combined with social media, texts, and emails, has conditioned us to believe that we must always be available to anyone. Like machines, we are taught that we need to be "on" all the time. Taking a break is frowned upon, and asking for help is often downright demonized. Saying no is looked upon as a selfish and self-centered act, especially for people who identify as women, though nobody is exempt from the expectation of endless

---

* David, Larry, Jerry Seinfeld, and Peter Mehlman, writers. *Seinfeld*. Season 5, episode 9, "The Masseuse." Directed by Tom Cherones. Aired November 18, 1993. https://www.netflix.com/ca/title/70153373.

performance in our culture. Even people who identify as white men are conditioned to work twelve hour days or multiple jobs in order to be "good providers." We are all conditioned to believe that our worth is determined by how much money we have, how many things we buy, how many followers we have on our social platforms, and how booked and busy we are. Whether you're an employee, a parent, or a community activist, you are expected to give of your time, energy, and resources enthusiastically, even if you're already overworked and exhausted. Not everyone who buys into this system would self-identify as a "people pleaser," but essentially, if you are trying to adhere to the expectations of a culture that has no respect for leisure, self-reflection, or boundaries, the result is the same.

People pleasing is, of course, not to be confused with generosity. When you are generous, you choose to give from your overflow. You give without expecting anything in return. People pleasing, on the other hand, causes one to overgive. When you overgive, you do so from a place of obligation or fear of disapproval or failure. You give because it's something you believe you must do. While generosity produces a sense of satisfaction, people pleasing results in one feeling beleaguered and resentful.

Your Inner Oppressor uses people pleasing to ensure that you're liked, accepted, and honored. Some patrons who have done this prompt share that they didn't realize that their need to be liked was a people-pleasing tactic. They struggled with stating their needs because, as a child, they were humiliated, ridiculed, or chastised for doing so. One patron shared that their sibling would be punished for being loud and disruptive. This taught them to act in a pleasant and agreeable way so they would receive their parents' love. The patron could now make the connection between their people-pleasing ways and the socialization they received when they were younger.

Multiple factors contribute to becoming a people pleaser. You may find that in certain situations and with certain people, you can easily be swayed, while in other situations, you can easily say no. At the core of your people-pleasing ways is a need to avoid rejection. You're hoping that people will fall in love with what you do to shield yourself from being rejected for who you are. Trying to address your people-pleasing ways can bring up all the feels.* You may feel an intense reaction in your body, or you may recall a

---

* In the years I've helped patrons and workshop attendees work through their boundary issues, I have found that this can bring up some intense emotions. If you're unable to get through this prompt, or if

situation where you were manipulated or forced into doing what you just didn't want to do. Some overgive to hide their neurodivergent way of being. Patrons and workshop attendees who received a diagnosis of autism, Asperger's Syndrome, or Attention Deficit Hyperactive Disorder (ADHD) as adults identified that they would be accommodating to others when they were the ones who needed accommodating. As children, they processed information in unique ways and interacted with people differently than others. Without a diagnosis as a child, they were often confused by how their parents and others in authority treated them. In this case, they would push aside their requests and say they were okay just so people would not express impatience or frustration.

For some, pleasing people develops because they don't know where they begin and the other person ends. This can be true of those who identify as intuitive, empathic, or as a Highly Sensitive Person (HSP). People who identify this way feel other people's emotions deeply. Those who identify as sensitive or intuitive cannot do boisterous forms of activism, such as marches, sit-ins, and protests. The loud shouts and intense energy from the crowd overstimulate their nervous systems. However, due to peer pressure, those who identify as Highly Sensitive or intuitive will say "yes" to these visible forms of activism just to please others.

By agreeing to engage in forms of activism that are not in alignment with their innate nature, a person from a Historically Desired Group (HDG) may abandon social justice causes, using their sensitivities or intuition as an excuse not to engage. Sitting at home and writing postcards to prospective voters in an area with voter suppression laws is less "glamorous" or visible than loudly shouting at a march or a protest. Letter writing, however, is just as impactful, especially for those with gentle, quiet, and highly sensitive personalities. Yet, due to our socialization, we seek ways to constantly make ourselves visible to receive approval, discouraging some from engaging in less visible and quieter forms of activism.

Being a people pleaser can mean that a person from an HDG will abandon the quest to challenge the dominant culture due to their fear of confrontation, criticism, rejection, or a lack of immediate rewards or instant gratification. Some may also feel resentment that they have to speak for a Historically

---

doing so brings up intense memories that you're unable to work through on your own, seek the help of a licensed therapist or mental health counselor. You are not alone.

Undesired Group (HUG) when they cannot even speak up for themselves. This can lead to "whataboutism," where people in an HDG lose empathy for those in HUGs because their own needs are not being met. A recurring theme that emerged when patrons and workshop attendees did this prompt was resentment. They complained that they are not confident expressing their own needs, so how could they be expected to do so for others. As empaths who are always anticipating the needs of others, they wonder who will speak up for them. They want to align with justice; however, they can barely state their boundaries with ease, let alone for anyone else.

Boundaries, however, are not the same for all. If you identify as a HUG, people pleasing can feel, or even be, like a matter of survival. Your Inner Oppressor pressures you to people please to avoid identity-based oppression, such as racism, Islamophobia. transphobia, homophobia, sexism, ableism, classism, and other identity-based -isms and -phobias. Women reluctantly give their number to a pushy man so they can walk away safely. A gay man may laugh at homophobic jokes to protect himself from harassment. Some Black people who have large frames are extra sweet when around non-Black people, so they appear less threatening (you read about this on Day 16—Body Insecurity).

One the one hand, HUGs have learned that relaxing one's boundaries can be used as a shield against identity-based oppression. If they smile excessively, laugh at humorless or insensitive jokes, and always say "yes" when asked to volunteer, then maybe they'll remain safe and protected. On the other hand, being available to anyone at any time leads to exploitation. In a culture that changes the rules depending on the social, ethnic, biological, and behavioral identities (SEBBIs) the person holds, when HUGs do establish boundaries around their time, resources, attention, and energy, they can be met with ridicule, scorn, and even violence. A workshop attendee who is of Latin descent shared that on a work team where she's one of two women, she is often asked to do administrative tasks, even though she shares the same job title as her male peers. Getting coffee, doing meeting minutes, and booking appointments for her boss and the rest of the team made her feel angry. She started to push back against the extra duties, and when she did, she was met with hostility.

Despite how others may react to your boundaries, creating them around your time, resources, attention, and energy is a beautiful thing. Leslie, a patron of European descent, explained how doing the self-reflective art in this prompt helped her move through her fear of designing her "inner border" (another name I use for boundaries) using the imagery of a garden:

My initial thought is that boundaries create clarity. I added a plant to show that there's a space for growth within boundaries. Organisms have specific bounds of what they need to survive. For example, if there is too much sun, some plants will die. So, plants teach us that if they get too much or too little of something, they won't survive. Then I drew a blue boundary around the entire photo in a pretty blue color showing that boundaries are beautiful.

Another patron, Rita, used the metaphor of a house to help her understand why creating boundaries is so important to her.

I started drawing a pink square and then it became a house. I stay inside the house and I get to decide who I will let in. Some are allowed in the garden in the front of my house. Others can peek in through the window. Some can greet me at the door. I had memories of people who invaded my boundaries, and so conceptualizing my inner border in the shape of the house where I can choose how to decorate it and what colors to choose made me feel better about my boundaries.

For some, their boundaries are too strong. Their inner border is a rigid barrier keeping everything out. This is what another patron, Jane, recognized when she looked at her boundary drawn as a labyrinth:

I remember someone saying that if you're feeling isolated, your boundaries are too much, and if you're feeling overwhelmed, your boundaries are too little. So, I guess I'm feeling really isolated because I drew my inner border as a labyrinth. It represents that there are a lot of pathways to get to me, and I can open some of those pathways up so I can feel more connected to others.

Some patrons made two drawings to represent the two sides of their boundaries. This was the case for Maggie:

I did two drawings. My first one reflected how I feel when all these demands come my way. It's like a wind that stirs up my energy—and not in a good way. I feel as if all these lines are swirling around me, leaving my chest feeling as if it's tightening. Then, I grabbed a second page. I still have the energy coming in from the side, but it hits the boundary. The demands, instead of overpowering me, bounce back towards where it came from. Then, I'm able to be colorful and big and be a blessing to people. As I drew the second image, the one with boundaries, I felt expansion in my heart. I could be all the colors instead of just settling on one.

Patrons and workshop attendees who identify with HUGs tend to report that they are honoring their ancestors when doing this prompt. Colonialism, imperialism, genocide, persecution, and other traumatic historical events, such as the Holocaust, chattel slavery, and land theft, robbed their ancestors from being able to set limits to their time, energy, abilities, and resources. HUGs often set boundaries not just for personal needs but also to do what their ancestors were not able to do.

What Is Possible When You Release Being a People Pleaser

Your voice becomes stronger. When you lack healthy, life-affirming boundaries, it is often a sign of not knowing who you are. Having healthy, life-affirming boundaries is one way to replace your people-pleasing ways. If you're not able to speak up for yourself and your needs, it'll be difficult doing so for others (and only if they invite you to do so). You will also gain the discernment to recognize when to speak up versus when you are doing so performatively because you hope for accolades and kudos from others.

Activism becomes more focused. You cannot join every cause, campaign, or charity. Knowing your deeply held values will enable you to easily say "no" without shame or guilt simply because you know what you're saying "yes" to. While we can expand our compassion to many causes and people at once, we ultimately need to choose a limited number of things that are most important to us (e.g., some may choose anti-racist work, others work for the environment, others to helping the unhoused or to LGBTQIA+ activism, etc.) that we can devote significant time and labor to.

Ancestors are honored. If there is a traumatic historical event that has interrupted your lineage, having boundaries honors those who came before you.

Colonialism, genocide, chattel slavery, internment camps, Holocaust, religious persecution, Holodomor, apartheid, forced relocation, and residential schools are just some of the intergenerational traumas that affected our ancestors. Those impacted by these atrocities had no ability to make choices in their own lives or to have boundaries respected and were treated as less than human. Being able to recognize and say no to exploitation in any form, and to value yourself and your choices, is one way to heal your bloodline.

Guided Self-Reflective Activities

Step 1—Identify your mood before starting. Go to page 239 and use the Mood Tracker to capture how you're feeling.

Step 2—My Inner Border (15 minutes).

Supplies needed: Colored markers or pens, timer.
What to do: ✄ Set your timer to count down from 15 minutes. ✄ Doodle or draw a metaphor for boundaries until the timer goes off.

Use the space below to complete My Inner Border.

Step 3—Journal (15 minutes).

Supplies needed: Sketchbook or journal, pen/pencil OR keyboard and screen, timer.

What to do:

- Navigate the prompt using GPS (see page 237).
- Set your timer to count down from 15 minutes.
- Capture the ramblings of your Inner Oppressor in your journal or sketchbook using the following prompts as a guide:

Prompt #1: Name your physical, emotional, sexual, mental, spiritual, and intellectual boundaries. List as many as you can. If you had difficulty putting this list together, how can you make it easier?

Prompt #2: How do you know if your boundaries have been crossed? Do you get angry? Do you get quiet? Do you let the other person know? Do you express your needs? If so, or if not, why?

Prompt #3: What is the one thing you would like to change so you can free up an hour of your day to focus on you and the causes you believe in?

Step 4—Track your mood after completing the Guided Self-Reflective Activities. Go to page 239 and use the Mood Tracker to capture how you're feeling now that you're done.

Congratulations!

You have completed today's actions. Please resist the urge to move quickly to the next day's actions. If you have capacity, you can also file your Summary Report at https://summary.innerfieldtrip.com (optional). Otherwise, go to page 243 and color in the day that you completed on the Journey Tracker page, put the Inner Field Trip aside, get on with your day, then resume tomorrow at the time you booked to meet with your Inner Oppressor.

Explore Appropriation

In October 2011, a student organization at Ohio University called Students Teaching About Racism in Society (STARS) launched a poster campaign entitled We're a Culture, Not a Costume.* Each poster featured a young adult with a somber face holding a photo of someone who was dressed as a stereotype about that young person's race, ethnicity, gender, class, or nationality. Over the years, reminders have been shared on socials using the hashtag #mycultureisnotacostume in the days leading up to Halloween, pleading with people not to darken their skin, wear a sombrero, or don a headscarf or feathered headdress as Halloween costumes, as these are culturally insensitive actions.

The pleas, however, often go ignored. Year after year, more examples are shared of people taking someone's culture and wearing it for one night as a costume. The harmful effects of cultural appropriation extend beyond Halloween. Sports teams use damaging stereotypes of Historically Undesired Groups (HUGs) as team mascots. In 2020, the Washington football team that's part of the National Football League in the United States finally changed their mascot name after decades of activism led by Amanda Blackhorse.** There are still hundreds of professional, college, and high school sports teams using slurs and stereotypes referring to Indigenous people, tribes, and nations as part of their team names.*** The reason it is so difficult to gain traction in terms of changing names or mascots that are offensive is

---

* See https://www.ohio.edu/orgs/stars/Poster_Campaign.html for the original campaign.

** See more about Blackhorse at https://www.womenshistory.org/education-resources/biographies/amanda-blackhorse.

*** See the statistics at https://fivethirtyeight.com/features/hundreds-of-schools-are-still-using-native-americans-as-team-mascots/.

that members of Historically Desired Groups (HDGs) often defend the use of such appropriated stereotypes as "tradition." Arguing that something should remain the same because that is how it has been for a long time is not a valid argument, especially when the tradition is at the expense of real people in the here and now.

Some issues of cultural appropriation and stereotyping need to be questioned, even if they arise, not out of callousness but out of a desire for growth and spiritual exploration. Yoga, which originated in India, has gone from a spiritual tradition focused on meditation to one that focuses on physical poses and merchandising. Yes, yoga is for everyone; however, non–South Asians are all too often the ones getting famous for being yoga gurus. Many self-styled gurus and influencers may add a small bit of traditional yoga into a New Age regimen yet are seen as yoga experts by those who do not have the skills and knowledge for cultural discernment. This results in the core tenets of yoga being watered down and becoming disassociated with its roots. A movement has emerged where some South Asians are highly invested in raising awareness about the ways yoga has been appropriated. Susanna Barkataki, who wrote *Embrace Yoga's Roots: Courageous Ways to Deepen Your Yoga Practice*, teaches people how to practice yoga without appropriating it. A return to honoring yoga's roots and recognizing that it's an age-old practice is one way to appreciate, and not appropriate, yoga.

Not only is culture appropriated, but so, too, are words and ideas. Otherwise known as intellectual appropriation, some HDGs use phrases, artistic ideas, and innovations created by HUGs without attribution. The dominant culture socializes us to believe that imitation is the best form of flattery. Imitation, however, feels more like theft when the counterfeit is monetizing what was copied from someone else. A patron shared the swirl of emotions she went through after a friend posted artwork that appeared to be in the artistic style of some Indigenous painters. When she brought up to her friend that as a non-Indigenous person, he should credit the Indigenous painters he learned from, he dismissed her inquiry by saying that it would be difficult for him to name his influencers due to him emulating different styles.

In an age of quick hits, fast posts, and clever memes, most fail to do research to find the originator. Quotes are posted without attribution, video clips are remixed without giving credit, and dance moves are copied without citing who inspired them. Phrases coined by academics such as Kimberlé Crenshaw's "intersectionality" and Moya Bailey's "misogynoir" have been co-opted and remixed to the point where Bailey said in an interview that others sometimes are credited for the word she coined.*

The appropriation of culture, ideas, creativity, and spiritual traditions signals that a person is lost. When this theft is condoned and encouraged at an interpersonal and institutional level, it represents a culture that is aimless and purposeless. At the core of appropriation is theft. Stealing another person's culture, words, and stories, even if it is in the form of a joke, is a way to deflect from a deep longing for meaning and purpose. This void or emptiness was noted by a patron, Cora, who did this prompt.

> Cultural appropriation happens when white people (like me) have felt empty of culture, like there is nothing to draw from, only whiteness which essentially is void of real culture. We have then used and clutched at other peoples' cultures and spirituality to glimpse some sense of belonging, often to the detriment of those cultures that have received nothing, or worse than nothing, in return. Real cultural appreciation would be to rediscover our own ancestry, spiritual sources, and diverse traditions (which is not the same for all white people) to draw from and to appreciate the richness of differences between cultures and have healthy and mutual exchanges without neediness.

The color of your skin isn't a culture. White skin isn't a culture just like Black skin isn't a culture. There may be history associated with the creation of whiteness or Blackness, but there is no *heritage*. Race was invented to create a hierarchy of superiority and inferiority based on nothing more than the shade of a person's skin. No one should want to claim a culture that's based on dehumanization, exploitation, superiority, or inferiority.

When considering Cora's words, we need to understand why so many Europeans who immigrated to settler nations, such as the United States, Brazil, Canada, Argentina, St. Vincent, Barbuda, the Dominican Republic, Australia, New Zealand, and South Africa, abandoned their ancestry of origin.**

---

* Bailey, Moya and Trudy. "On Misogynoir: Citation, Erasure, and Plagiarism." *Feminist Media Studies* 18, no. 4 (July 4, 2018): 762–768. https://doi.org/10.1080/14680777.2018.1447395.

** Indigenous people and people of African descent in the Americas were forced to give up their cultures as a means of control. In most cases, legislation was passed in settler nations to prevent Indigenous and African people from speaking their languages, giving themselves culturally significant names, eating culturally relevant foods, and dressing in culturally relevant clothing. It was a

Most did so to fit into the dominant culture and avoid discrimination and isolation. Patrons and workshop attendees have shared sad stories of grandparents not teaching their parents Spanish, Italian, Yiddish, French, or Gaelic, just to name a few, and the loss of connection to their ancestors since the language and related traditions were not passed on.

The dominant culture benefits from the flatlining of culture and cultural traditions of various ethnicities to create a supermajority of white people in certain countries or on certain continents. White supremacy would be more difficult to uphold if each ethnic group that is categorized as white saw themselves as being different from one another. If a French American and an Irish American perceived themselves as culturally different, each adhering strongly to their own rituals, languages, spiritual traditions, and costumes, it would become harder to "other" an African American who is also culturally diverse from them.

The flatlining of culture in majority white settler nations in general, and in the American population in particular, is a political tool to create the illusion of homogeneity and cohesiveness so as to form a power block. While a patron like Cora may not realize the reason she feels so divorced from having a culture of her own, make no mistake that this has been a centuries-long effort to create an *Us vs. Them* mentality, in which white people feel aligned with one another based on the color of their skin alone. Many cultural critics and writers have discussed some variation on this in their work, such as Jess Row in *White Flights: Race, Fiction, and the American Imagination*.

What makes up a culture is its foods, customs, language, art, literature, symbols, religion or spiritual practices, and social values. Culture should make people come alive through song, dance, festivals, and shared rituals. We all, no matter how far back we go into our pasts, have strong cultures of origin. Even if your family immigrates to a new nation, you will mix elements of your ancestry of origin with the culture of the country where you reside. If your lineage lost their culture over the past few generations, you can revive those cultural traditions with a little bit of research. There is no need to appropriate someone else's culture to find meaning. Instead, ask questions of the elders in

systematic effort to diminish the agency and autonomy of Indigenous and African people to steal their land and labor. For more on the pillars that prop up a system rooted in white supremacy culture, read "Heteropatriarchy and the Three Pillars of White Supremacy" by Andrea Smith, which you can find in the book *Feminist Theory Reader*, edited by Carole McCann, Seung-kyung Kim, and Emek Ergun.

your family, join cultural associations related to your ancestry of origin, and if you are financially able, visit the country where your ancestors came from.

One of the wonderful things about contemporary life is our access to information and diversity. If one ethnic group has a big festival, for example, or a section of a city that proliferates with their cuisine, others who are not part of that culture are implicitly invited to participate and learn what makes that culture unique. Culture connects us to our shared humanity and should foster an openness to learning, not an impulse to steal and claim ownership. If a culture exists only because it debases, diminishes, and dehumanizes others, then that is not a culture at all. It is, at best, appropriation (which may be done out of ignorance without ill-intent but still must be challenged) and, at worst, superiority or entitlement.

This is one reason why colonizers attack the culture of those who are indigenous to the lands they are invading. By removing people from their lands, making their customs illegal, and banning them from speaking their language, the cultural group's bond with one another is weakened. Unlike the purpose of flatlining ethnicities, which has at its center a goal of transforming all white people into one cohesive HDG, the eradication of indigenous cultures (and African cultures among the enslaved) was designed to scatter, confuse, and dehumanize HUGs.

Appropriation, sadly, is just another way to flatline culture. The person who wears another person's culture as a joke, uses cultural stereotypes to reflect the fighting spirit of a sports team, or fails to give attribution to the originator of an idea is reflecting what the dominant culture has done to them—robbed them of aliveness, fullness, and wholeness and replaced it with emptiness, bleakness, and senselessness.

If you want to become a better ancestor, you need to reject appropriation. No, this does not mean you are not allowed to go out for Chinese food, do yoga, appreciate the art of Frida Kahlo, or feel inspired by Martin Luther King Jr. That kind of rhetoric is exemplary of the hyperbole of those who wish to keep HDGs in power. By exaggerating and distorting what HUGs are asking for, HDGs can make their request sound extreme or ridiculous, giving them an excuse to reject or make fun of it. We are all allowed to appreciate and learn from one another. To be a better ancestor calls for mindfulness, discernment, and self-education.

One way to reject appropriation is to get into the habit of naming who you're learning from. Noting the source of something that enriches you, whether it be creative (e.g., artists, dancers, musicians), spiritual (e.g., shamans, pastors, rabbis, Imams, or Sufis), or intellectual (e.g., authors, academics, or theorists), should add to your appreciation, not detract from it. Credibility is established because people can trace where your influences and ideas come from. Citing the creative, spiritual, or intellectual lineage of the people, places, or things that matter to you improves your sense of self because you acknowledge that you are part of an impressive lineage of wisdom. You become a better ancestor and deepen your understanding of the cultures that have enriched your life when you identify who you're learning from. In addition, because you cared so much to name your creative, spiritual, and intellectual lineage, you set the example for your descendants to do the same to you so that you're never forgotten.

Appreciation of other people's cultures is often seen as the opposite of cultural appropriation. But if you treat culture like a mash-up without acknowledging its origin and view everything as "yours" to use as you choose without mindfulness, you may still be appropriating even if you are appreciating. Being respectful and informed about other cultures is one way to remove the dehumanizing cloak of cultural appropriation.

For this prompt, you will take a step away from issues around appropriation and appreciation of other cultures and instead focus on building an appreciation for *your own* culture. Remember it. Research it. Reconnect with it. Resurrect the languages, rituals, and customs that your ancestors shed to fit in with the dominant culture.

What Is Possible When You Release Appropriation

Halloween and sports events become safe and enjoyable for all. Dressing up as a superhero or inanimate object are just some of the options available as Halloween costumes. Mascots for sports teams can reflect the fighting spirit of animals and other symbols. If you want your next party to be safe for all, you will call out harmful mascots and costumes, or better yet, let others know in advance not to engage in this type of behavior at your gathering. That's what becoming a better ancestor is all about.

Self-satisfaction grows. Knowing that you belong to a culture that holds deep meaning can raise your self-esteem. The stories you tell become more dynamic and the joy you feel becomes infectious as you regale listeners with the tales of your cultural, creative, spiritual, and intellectual lineages.

Reclamation heals the bloodline. Your ancestors may have voluntarily or involuntarily given up their culture to align with the dominant culture.* You may go through some discomfort coming to terms with the actions of your ancestors; however, continued cultural disconnection deepens the intergenerational wounds. By reclaiming your cultural heritage and making a commitment to learn the language your ancestors once spoke, dance to the music your ancestors once sang, or cook the meals that your ancestors once prepared, you create a pathway of healing that your descendants can model.

Guided Self-Reflective Activities

Step 1—Identify your mood before starting. Go to page 239 and use the Mood Tracker to capture how you're feeling.

Step 2—Cherished Lineage (15 minutes).

	Supplies needed: Colored markers or pens, timer.
	What to do:
	✄ Set your timer to count down from 15 minutes.
	✄ Draw or doodle the foods, language, rituals, religion/spiritual practices, music, literature, art, and symbols associated with the culture or ethnicity of your ancestors.
	✄ If you are multicultural—in other words, if your ancestors come from two or more cultures—then choose one that holds the most interest to you.

---

* For some HUGs, their ancestors were forced to give up their culture due to the demands of and legislation passed by colonizers and settlers.

Use the space below to doodle or draw your Cherished Lineage.

Step 3—Journal (15 minutes).

Supplies needed: Sketchbook or journal, pen/pencil OR keyboard and screen, timer.

What to do:

- Navigate the prompt using GPS (see page 237).
- Set your timer to count down from 15 minutes.
- Capture the ramblings of your Inner Oppressor in your journal or sketchbook using the following prompts as a guide:

Prompt #1: What aspect of your ancestors' forgotten culture do you want to remember? What one action can you take towards putting your lineage's culture into practice? Will you sign up for language or cooking classes? Something else?

Prompt #2: What is the difference between appreciating someone's culture, ideas, or creations versus appropriating them? How can you make the distinction between the two?

Prompt #3: Have you (or someone you know) appropriated someone's culture, ideas, or creations? If yes, what can you see now that you couldn't see then? What is still unclear?

Step 4—Track your mood after completing the Guided Self-Reflective Activities. Go to page 239 and use the Mood Tracker to capture how you're feeling now that you're done.

Congratulations!

You have completed today's actions. Please resist the urge to move quickly to the next day's actions. If you have capacity, you can also file your Summary Report at https://summary.innerfieldtrip.com (optional). Otherwise, go to page 243 and color in the day that you completed on the Journey Tracker page, put the Inner Field Trip aside, get on with your day, then resume tomorrow at the time you booked to meet with your Inner Oppressor.

Active Rest Stop

*O*nce again, you've reached another Active Rest Stop, and they are built into the 30-day Inner Field Trip quest so that you take a moment to pause. You've encountered one on Day 11 and 15, another one today, and there will be one more on Day 25. To remind yourself why we take a moment to pause during the Inner Field Trip, go back and review Day 11.

What to Do During an Active Rest Stop

As a reminder, instead of reviewing the art or writings you produced during the previous three or four days, you will instead focus on creating, building, composing, moving, or making. Resmaa Menakem recommends discharging and dispersing energy nurtured through conflict or high-stress situations using movement, such as dance, playing sports, exercise, or physical labor.* Movement is encouraged during the Active Rest Stop, and so, too, are creative and artistic pursuits. The infographic on the following page gives some ideas on what you can do during the Active Rest Stop.

The font may be a bit small, so I've listed the six categories and related activities below:

- ✄ **Build It**—Building Blocks, Popsicle Sticks, Toothpicks, Glue Gun, Model Toy, Jigsaw Puzzle, Slime, Play-Doh, Mimetic Sand

- ✄ **Make It**—Knitting, Sewing, Crocheting, Needlepoint, Embroidery, Beading, Woodworking, Baking

---

* Menakem, Resmaa. *My Grandmother's Hands: Racialized Trauma and the Pathway to Mending Our Hearts and Bodies*. Las Vegas: Central Recovery Press (2017): Chapter 12.

ACTIVE REST STOP IDEAS

- ✄ **Illustrate It**—Painting, Drawing, Cartooning, Collaging, Junk Journaling, Diamond Painting, Lettering

- ✄ **Compose / Write It**—Music, Screenplay, Memoir, Pandemic Reflections, Creative Writing, TV Script, One-Person Show, Play, Poetry

- ✄ **Move It**—Walking, Hiking, Dancing, Cycling, Trampolining, Skating, Exercising

- ✄ **Reflect on It**—Meditating, Praying, Napping, Deep Breathing, Listening to Calm Music, Yoga, Bubble Bathing, Playing Calm Music on an Instrument

Some things to remember when engaging in an Active Rest Stop:

- ✄ You're not doing this to be seen, published, or applauded. In other words, let go of any expectation of what your creation could become. Just be in the creating mood.

⚒ It's best to do the activity solo, but if you want to include someone, choose someone with the most childlike personality. You don't want to do this with someone who's going to descend into criticism or complaints (whether directed at you or themselves).

⚒ The activity you choose for the Active Rest Stop can be the same one you do during the next one, or totally different.

⚒ Set the timer for 30 minutes and then let your creativity take over. Color outside the lines. Leave the mess on the floor. Play a wrong note. Write using run-on sentences. Use your nondominant hand to paint. Create a Play-Doh tree with red bark and purple leaves. Enjoy the messiness of the activity and release perfection.

Active Rest Stop Activities

Step 1—Identify your mood before starting. Go to page 239 and use the Mood Tracker Ring to capture how you're feeling.

Step 2—Engage in the Active Rest Stop (30 minutes).

	**Supplies needed:** Materials to engage in the Active Rest Stop, timer.
	What to do: ⚒ Choose one Active Rest Stop activity. ⚒ Take a few minutes to set up your play or studio space. ⚒ Start the timer, then engage in the activity until the timer goes off.

Step 3—Fill in the blanks. Once the timer goes off and before tidying up your play or studio space, complete the sentences below. Spend no more than 15 seconds on each question, and jot down some thoughts.

After engaging in the Active Rest Stop, my Inner Oppressor revealed:

_____

_____

_____

_____

It's no wonder because:

_____

_____

_____

_____

Therefore, the one action I will take is:

_____

_____

_____

_____

Step 4—Track your mood after completing the Guided Self-Reflective Activities. Go to page 239 and use the Mood Tracker Ring to capture how you're feeling now that you're done.

Congratulations!

You have completed today's actions. Please resist the urge to move quickly to the next day's actions. If you have capacity, you can also file your Summary Report at https://summary.innerfieldtrip.com (optional). Otherwise, go to page 243 and color in the day that you completed on the Journey Tracker page, put the Inner Field Trip aside, get on with your day, then resume tomorrow at the time you booked to meet with your Inner Oppressor.

Explore Weaponized Kindness

Compassion, empathy, and being sensitive are emotions some of us use to understand another person's suffering. If you can "walk in someone else's shoes," you'll have more clarity about that person's pain. Being kind and caring are gestures you can extend to someone else, especially if they've been wounded by identity-based oppression.

However, when kindness is used to silence, suppress, and shut down any conversation around systemic injustices and social inequities, then it's wielded as a tool to injure, manipulate, and gain an advantage. This is what I call "weaponized kindness," and it is a form of tone policing where one criticizes how someone is saying something instead of finding fault with the oppression or bias. A calm voice, sweet words, and a bright smile are used to deny, dismiss, or discard the lived experience of those who live with identity-based oppression. Often, the phrases used to weaponize kindness are:

- "Let's just be kind to each other."

- "Let's be civil."

- "If we lead with love, then this conflict will melt away."

- "Let's not let politics get in the way. Family comes first."

Genuine kindness is not the problem. When someone is expressing heartfelt kindness, they are friendly, warm, and helpful. They do not seek praise or reward for their courteous deeds and they also respect another person's need to speak up or share an experience or perspective. A person exhibiting kindness is concerned for others, no matter what the person looks like, and they give feedback to help the other person do better and are eager to do better themselves. Weaponized kindness, by contrast, criticizes and demeans with a smile. The person who is weaponizing kindness only extends grace if the wounded shares their social, ethnic, biological, and behavioral identities (SEBBIs for short). If someone is claiming that their philosophy is all based on love, kindness, and family, yet they are refusing to recognize the actual feelings of others who don't share their views, then this is a type of kindness intended to silence dissent.

At the core of weaponized kindness, ironically, is a lack of self-kindness. When self-kindness is high, it can easily be extended to others. Secure people are magnanimous and confident enough to listen to dissent without it fracturing their sense of self. When self-kindness and self-esteem are low, then so-called kindness may just be conformity or attention seeking. Your Inner Oppressor can be crafty and use weaponized kindness to make you appear good and special. This allows you to cast the spotlight on yourself instead of the people for whom you claim to be advocating. Some within the Inner Field Trip Basecamp have embarrassingly shared that they would do kind things for Historically Undesired Groups (HUGs) so they wouldn't be accused of racism. A patron who is white said that, while shopping, she would randomly approach a Black person and give them money as a goodwill gesture. However, her motivation was to use the act to prove to her friends that she was one of the good ones.

As you can see, falling over yourself to perform kindness for those who are not even seeking help just so others will "notice" is a form of people pleasing, too (discussed on Day 18). Not only do people from Historically Desired Groups (HDGs) use "selfless" acts to weaponize kindness, they may also use money for the same reason. Philanthropic groups and charities need money to do their work, yet some affluent people may donate to charities, not because the organization aligns with their deeply held values, but because donating is seen as a way to save and rescue HUGs. Although donating to valid organizations is not a "bad" thing, charitable acts do not require the giver to do the interpersonal work required to change power dynamics and stereotypes in their everyday lives. Giving hundreds of dollars to charities should not be used as a stand-in to avoid challenging oneself. A theme that some patrons identified after doing the prompts is that they use money to protect them from callouts. If they make a mistake, they hope that they'll be remembered for their financials contributions. Buying books written by HUGs, shopping at HUG-owned businesses, and purchasing seats to a workshop hosted by HUGs are some of the ways that HDGs use money as a shield.

The problem with this form of kindness is that what should be viewed as a fair exchange of value (money for a product or service) is confused with acts of benevolence, selflessness, and philanthropy. HUGs can sense when kindness has strings attached. This causes confusion, anger, and a sense of being infantilized. While dining at a restaurant with a friend, another Black woman, a white man approached, slammed a stack of cash on the table, told us he's paying for our meal, then walked away. My friend and I, both accomplished business owners, sat there utterly confused. He did not place money on anyone else's table, and we wondered why he singled us out. Did he give us the money because he thought that, as Black people, we couldn't afford our meal? We were going back and forth, trying to make sense of what he did, wondering if the money was funny, until we saw him put money on the table of a white couple who were dining on the other side of the room. That is when we relaxed. Perhaps he won the lottery and was feeling generous—who knows? And yet, look at the mental gymnastics we put ourselves through. We just could not separate the dynamics of race from what was supposedly a generous gesture. And that's all it was—an expression of kindness. However, due to our experience, we overanalyzed the gesture because we're so used to seeing people misuse kindness as a way to boost their ego.

For HUGs who were raised in collectivist cultures, kindness is used as a survival tactic. As a supposed Model Minority, South Asians, East Asians, Latin Americans, and Southeast Asians may weaponize kindness to show that they're better than Black people. Kindness is used to remain silent about oppression and appear peaceful, compliant, and disciplined. At its core is a need to be safe within a culture that harms them. The reality that many patrons realize is that civility and decorum used as a protective measure does nothing to stop identity-based oppression.

Kindness is also weaponized in who people choose to learn from. Some choose to be taught by anti-racism and anti-oppression educators who are soft spoken. While it's not an issue to favor those whose teaching style aligns with your learning style, it becomes a problem when the sole reason you chose that educator is because the way they deliver their message allows you to never feel uncomfortable (a concept I call "tone filtering"). A few patrons shared that they were unaware that their rejection of certain anti-racism educators may be rooted in anti-Blackness. One patron said that oppression is harsh enough; she doesn't need to feel the same harshness from educators to make her feel even more guilty about her advantages. Once she became aware of tone filtering, this patron wondered about the voices and experiences she was missing out on because she only wanted to learn from kind, soft-spoken, and eloquent educators.

Some go as far as to use tone filtering as a way to pit HUGs against each other. In 2018, I observed a post by a white woman who praised the teaching style of half a dozen anti-racism educators. If she had stopped there, no one would've had a problem with her post. However, she decided to critique the teaching style of anti-racism educators she didn't like and amplified stereotypes about Black women. This is why tone filtering is dangerous. It can intentionally or unintentionally lead HDGs to create friction between HUGs as they rate kindness through the dominant culture's lens.

What Is Possible When You Stop Weaponizing Kindness

You protect your empathy. Weaponized kindness causes you to overgive to the point where you deplete your financial, emotional, and physical resources. Feeling drained can lead to numbness and indifference. When you show kindness in a healthy way, you reserve your energy for the social causes that need your attention, thus protecting your empathy.

You give people the space to arrive at a solution that works for them. People often know what to do in most situations—if you allow them to think for themselves. When you weaponize kindness, you remove a person's agency by trying to rescue and save them. Patronizing people only builds resentment. Being in solidarity with those who face identity-based oppression is a healthy way to show kindness because this recognizes their humanity, independence, and autonomy.

Guided Self-Reflective Activities

Step 1—Identify your mood before starting. Go to page 239 and use the Mood Tracker to capture how you're feeling.

Step 2—Imagining Kindness (15 minutes).

Supplies needed: Colored markers or pens, timer.

What to do:
- Set your timer to count down from 15 minutes.
- Without using a ruler, draw as many squares using as many colors as you can on the blank page before the timer goes off.

**Use the space below to draw, doodle,
or illustrate Imagining Kindness.**

Step 3—Journal (15 minutes).

Supplies needed: Sketchbook or journal, pen/pencil OR keyboard and screen, timer.

What to do:

- Navigate the prompt using GPS (see page 237).
- Set your timer to count down from 15 minutes.
- Capture the ramblings of your Inner Oppressor in your journal or sketchbook using the following prompts as a guide:

Prompt #1: Who has modeled kindness as a weapon, and who has modeled kindness as a true character trait?

Prompt #2: Recall a time you used kindness to dismiss a marginalized person's lived experience with systemic oppression or to disengage from aligning with oppressed people. What did you say? What did you do? How did the other person react?

Prompt #3: In what ways do you use kindness to hide your fear of making mistakes and appearing less than perfect, especially in anti-racist and anti-oppressive communities?

Step 4—Track your mood after completing the Guided Self-Reflective Activities. Go to page 239 and use the Mood Tracker to capture how you're feeling now that you're done.

Congratulations!

You have completed today's actions. Please resist the urge to move quickly to the next day's actions. If you have capacity, you can also file your Summary Report at https://summary.innerfieldtrip.com (optional). Otherwise, go to page 243 and color in the day that you completed on the Journey Tracker page, put the Inner Field Trip aside, get on with your day, then resume tomorrow at the time you booked to meet with your Inner Oppressor.

Explore Imposter Phenomenon

*T*here is an episode of *Frasier* where the title character, Dr. Frasier Crane, is overcome with self-doubt and self-criticism after getting news that he will be receiving a lifetime achievement award for his work as a radio psychiatrist.* Dr. Crane visits his former supervisor, whom he had not seen in close to 25 years. Although his mentor assures Dr. Crane that he deserves the award, Frasier ends up missing the awards ceremony, slumped on a set of stairs just outside his mentor's office.

A lack of self-confidence and low self-esteem when you're otherwise accomplished, credentialed, and capable is what has become known as "imposter syndrome." Originally called "imposter phenomenon" by Pauline Rose Clance and Suzanne Imes who coined the phrase in the late 1970s, it was developed after the two psychologists observed that high-achieving women tend to feel like phonies despite outstanding abilities. "Women who experience the imposter phenomenon persist in believing that they are really not bright and have fooled anyone who thinks otherwise."** Although imposter syndrome was initially observed in women, research has shown that it also affects men*** and is observed in students, surgeons, entrepreneurs, nurses, actors, lawyers, and CEOs (just to name a few).

---

* *Frasier*. (2001) Season 8, Episode 9, "Frasier's Edge." Directed by David Lee. Aired January 9, 2001, on Crave. https://www.crave.ca/en/tv-shows/frasier/frasiers-edge-s8e9.

** Clance, Pauline Rose, and Suzanne Ament Imes. "The Imposter Phenomenon in High Achieving Women: Dynamics and Therapeutic Intervention." *Psychotherapy: Theory, Research & Practice* 15, no. 3 (1978): 241–247. https://doi.org/10.1037/h0086006.

*** Common sense and studies would also lead us to conclude that this could only be amplified for trans and nonbinary folks.

In this chapter, I'll be using the term "imposter phenomenon" as Clance and Imes intended. "Syndrome" denotes that something is medically wrong with the person. The American Psychological Association defines "syndrome" as "a set of signs that are usually due to a single cause (or set of related causes) and together indicate a particular physical or mental disease or disorder."[*] Feeling like a fraud, con artist, trickster, sham, fake, or cheat when you are otherwise very capable isn't an affliction to be cured or a disease that needs treatment. Nor is imposter phenomenon a personality defect or a failed character trait. It is a systematic and deeply entrenched societal effort to undermine very capable and accomplished people by making them believe that their feelings of fraud are an individual failing. Ruchika Tulshyan and Jodi-Ann Burey write that "imposter syndrome puts the blame on individuals, without accounting for the historical and cultural contexts that are foundational to how it manifests. Imposter syndrome directs our view toward fixing women at work instead of fixing the places where women work."[**]

The dominant culture uses imposter phenomenon to distract you from looking at the structural issues that contribute to feelings of low self-worth. In partnership with your Inner Oppressor, the dominant culture socializes you to feel like a con artist, fake, fraud, cheat, deceiver, and trickster despite having the talents, abilities, gifts, and skills to complete the task or project. You can find no shortage of videos, podcasts, and articles giving tips on how to fix feeling like a fraud or trickster in the workplace. Yet, very few identify systemic oppression as a contributor to imposter phenomenon.

Before continuing, I want to point out that there's a difference between mistrust in one's abilities and misrepresenting one's experiences. The latter is about creating a persona to trick people into believing that you have experiences and skills that you did not earn or possess. For example, some claim Indigenous or African ancestry to gain access to prominent positions and/or prestigious grants.[***] Some politicians and job seekers inflate their resumes to make it appear that they worked at respected companies, held reputable

---

[*] American Psychological Association, s.v. "Syndrome," accessed January 19, 2023. https://dictionary.apa.org/syndrome.

[**] Tulshyan, Ruchika, and Jodi-Ann Burey. "Stop Telling Women They Have Imposter Syndrome," *Harvard Business Review* (February 11, 2021). https://hbr.org/2021/02/stop-telling-women-they-have-imposter-syndrome.

[***] For example, "pretendian," a combination of "pretending" and "Indian," refers to those who falsely claim Indigenous ancestry. There are, unfortunately, too many examples to cite, but a search of "pretendian" in a search engine will (sadly) reveal many results.

jobs, and graduated from prestigious schools. Some in the wellness and self-improvement community claim abilities they do not possess to build their clientele or influencer status for economic gains. Lying about your credentials so you can appear more than is not the same as hiding what you already possess so you can seem less than.

The function of imposter phenomenon is to cause you to mistrust your abilities, feel as if you don't belong, and labor excessively to satisfy expectations you'll never be able to reach. An example of this can be found in corporate culture. Since so-called "masculine" traits such as assertiveness, toughness, and strength are prized in leadership, when a woman is promoted to a leadership position, she may feel out of place because she's been socialized to be nurturing, empathetic, and vulnerable.[*] As she navigates her new position, she will have to adopt masculine traits[**] to fit into her role, which then causes her to worry that she'll be found out. It goes without saying, however, that once this woman adapts herself to behave in ways patriarchal culture sees as more "masculine," she will be criticized—often by men and other women alike—for not being "feminine" enough.

The need to do more to meet unrealistic expectations has always been a reality for Historically Undesired Groups (HUGs). Due to classicism, ableism, sexism, racism, and imperialism, some have had their labor extracted, plundered, and stolen as those in Historically Desired Groups (HDGs) took credit. Even today, when many in HUGs have risen to positions of prominence, they are constantly under pressure to overperform and believe their output isn't good enough.[***]

If you spend too much time laboring to prove your worth due to a fear of being found out, then you'll pay less attention to dismantling systemic oppression and structural barriers. This bears repeating, whether one is an attorney attempting to make partner in a law firm or a stay-at-home mother

---

[*] Feenstra, Sanne, Christopher T. Begeny, Michelle K. Ryan, Floor A. Rink, Janka I. Stoker, and Jennifer Jordan. "Contextualizing the Impostor 'Syndrome.'" *Frontiers in Psychology* 11 (2020). https://www.frontiersin.org/articles/10.3389/fpsyg.2020.575024.

[**] Masculine versus feminine energies are based on an either/or framework that doesn't consider gender fluid, nonbinary, nonconforming, transgender, and other gender identities. I use the term "masculine traits" only because it is what was used in the journal article that I'm referencing.

[***] For a discussion of this, see Roxane Gay's "The Price of Black Ambition," an essay in the *Virginia Quarterly Review*.

who strives to attain the near impossible standards set by our culture of what makes a "good mother": HUGs overexerting themselves to prove their basic worthiness zaps their energy and distracts them from actively dismantling the systems that have made them feel unworthy in the first place. Hence, while there is no one person, or even one political party, to "blame" for systemic imposter phenomenon, toxic patriarchy, white supremacy, capitalism, ableism, and heteronormativity coexist to actively suppress, depress, and oppress HUGs.

As stated, imposter phenomenon is not just experienced by women. Men, too, can experience imposter phenomenon, especially those who are affected by systemic poverty. Patrons who identify as men, no matter their class status, reported feeling less capable when they do not receive external validation from peers, coworkers, family members, or friends. In a way, their feelings of not being acknowledged cause them to not be aware of the pain others are enduring. Even if they enjoy advantages due to the intersection of their skin color and gender, some men are unable to advocate for HUGs because they are distracted by trying to prove their worth so they can receive praise, gain power, and earn profits. Keeping so many people feeling like imposters due to not receiving recognition of their worthiness or praise for their efforts is exactly what the dominant culture needs to thrive. If HDGs and HUGs are unable to unite in a shared cause, then the dominant culture is never challenged.

For HUGs, imposter phenomenon tends to emerge due to challenging known stereotypes about their social, ethnic, biological, and behavioral identities (SEBBIs). Some HUGs have been socialized to believe they are unintelligent and lazy. HUGs are often criticized for the very things that HDGs are praised for. To make matters more complex, when HUGs do achieve something, they may feel guilty. Self-criticism arises when they attain personal success, but their community is still mired in identity-based oppression. For example, a patron, who is Iranian, felt bad knowing that people in her homeland are fighting for freedom with their lives while she gets to focus on completing graduate studies far away from the conflict.

Imposter phenomenon causes mothers to downplay their roles. Mothers already spend immense amounts of emotional and physical labor raising their children. The dominant culture still deems it necessary to criticize their efforts. It was while doing this prompt that Brittany Carmona-Holt, author of *Tarot for*

Pregnancy: A Companion for Radical Magical Birthing Folks, realized that gentle parenting* is, in fact, a form of activism:

> Raising my son to see his full humanity, honoring his motives and perspective, and not acting out punitively when he makes a mistake will hopefully mean that he'll grow up to not be fragile when he's called out for mistakes he makes. This realization comes at a timely moment in my life when a reinvigorated commitment to all the ways in which I show up for the revolution has taken me away from showing up as my best self as a parent. I needed to remember that not traumatizing him around his mistakes is a part of how I'm contributing to the revolution too.

Negative self-talk was cited over and over by patrons and workshop attendees as a companion to imposter phenomenon. Feeling that you don't deserve the good things you achieved is encouraged by unhealthy internal chatter. It's as if your Inner Oppressor and Inner Critic have teamed up to remind you of all the ways you're a failure and fraud. One patron said that her negative self-talk is cruel while another said they would never say to someone the things they say to themself. You are not born with a nattering nabob of negativity in your head. Situations in your life can produce a deep vocabulary of self-blame and low self-worth. Sayaka, a patron who was adopted, reflects on how that experience affected how she speaks to herself:

> I watched a talk about adoption trauma that helped me see very clearly that I've NEVER really felt that I truly belonged anywhere. As a child, I was taught that I was not okay due to being given up at birth and then living in a foster home for a year before being adopted. Negative self-worth, shame, and low self-worth is literally how I started and set the course for the rest of my life. I need more than anything else to focus on healing this trauma to get to a place of self-trust.

The patrons you have met in this chapter demonstrate that imposter phenomenon isn't simply flaws that an individual can fix on their own. Feeling like a fraud when you have the capabilities and credentials to perform the task

---

* See https://www.verywellfamily.com/what-is-gentle-parenting-5189566 for an overview of gentle parenting.

can only be considered in relation to culture and socialization. If HDGs and HUGs are teetering in self-doubt due to the unrealistic expectations that the dominant culture places on them, then imposter phenomenon must be a concern for all.

What Is Possible When You Release Imposter Phenomenon

Self-worth grows. Taking inventory of your achievements and experiences helps to disarm the hold the dominant culture has on you. You start focusing on your strengths and stop wasting time laboring over your weaknesses.

Trust in others is established. When you remind yourself of your deep wisdom and knowledge, you improve your self-worth. When you can trust yourself, it makes it easier to trust others. This is something that's needed to create communities of belonging where all voices are heard.

The connection between individual and systemic is made. You have been trained to believe that imposter phenomenon is a personal failing. Feeling like a fraud or con when you're otherwise capable could not happen without the contributions of unrealistic external demands. When you can finally see that systemic issues contribute to feelings of low self-worth and that capitalism feeds off your need to overwork just to prove yourself, you'll finally be free of imposter phenomenon.

Guided Self-Reflective Activities

Step 1—Identify your mood before starting. Go to page 239 and use the Mood Tracker to capture how you're feeling.

Step 2—Wisdom Word Cloud (15 minutes).

<table>
<tr>
<td rowspan="2"></td>
<td>Supplies needed: Pen, markers, crayons, timer.</td>
</tr>
<tr>
<td>

What to do:
- Set your timer to count down from 15 minutes.
- In a nonlinear way, write down as many personal and professional achievements, accomplishments, and awards that you have received over the past few years.
- If you have time, draw a line around the words, making it look similar to a cloud. Use your favorite color to color it in.

</td>
</tr>
</table>

Use the space below to draw or doodle your Wisdom Word Cloud.

Step 3—Journal (15 minutes).

Supplies needed: Sketchbook or journal, pen/pencil OR keyboard and screen, timer.

What to do:

- Navigate the prompt using GPS (see page 237).
- Set your timer to count down from 15 minutes.
- Capture the ramblings of your Inner Oppressor in your journal or sketchbook using the following prompts as a guide:

Prompt #1: How does the achievement or accomplishment contribute to your intellectual lineage? What lessons does it teach you about the depth of your wisdom?

Prompt #2: What is the common theme that draws your wisdom together? How can you use it for clues around your zone of genius?

Prompt #3: Look at each word within your Wisdom Word Cloud. What sensations are you observing in your body? What does this tell you about what you're seeing, sensing, or feeling?

Step 4—Track your mood after completing the Guided Self-Reflective Activities. Go to page 239 and use the Mood Tracker to capture how you're feeling now that you're done.

Congratulations!

You have completed today's actions. Please resist the urge to move quickly to the next day's actions. If you have capacity, you can also file your Summary Report at https://summary.innerfieldtrip.com (optional). Otherwise, go to page 243 and color in the day that you completed on the Journey Tracker page, put the Inner Field Trip aside, get on with your day, then resume tomorrow at the time you booked to meet with your Inner Oppressor.

Explore Sibling Dynamics

Olivia de Havilland and Joan Fontaine were biological sisters who just did not get along. Born just over a year apart, the sisters became actors and starred in some of Hollywood's biggest films in the 1930s, '40s, and '50s. Although Fontaine entered acting after her sister, she was the first between the two to win an Academy Award in 1941 for Best Actress.[*] Their sibling rivalry came into focus when Fontaine ignored de Havilland's outstretched hand when the former went onstage to accept the Oscar. In her autobiography, Fontaine says that she did not see her sister's hand, as she was frozen with shock at winning.[**] Despite their conflict that lasted decades, when Fontaine died in 2013, de Havilland said she was saddened by her sister's death.[***]

Such are the dynamics of sibling relationships. Fame and wealth do not shield someone from having a difficult relationship with siblings. In some cases, siblings can be a source of love, hope, and happiness, or they can be a source of bitterness, hostility, and pain. Both can also be true. Siblings represent the first platonic, nonromantic relationship we will form and are often the longest relationship we'll have in our families. Researchers found that children who live with their siblings will spend 50 percent of their free time with them.[****]

---

[*] See https://www.oscars.org/oscars/ceremonies/1941/R?qt-honorees=1.

[**] Fontaine, Joan. *No Bed of Roses: An Autobiography.* New York: William Morrow. (1978): 136.

[***] See https://www.cbsnews.com/news/olivia-de-havilland-shocked-and-saddened-by-sister-joan -fontaines-death/.

[****] Dunifon, Rachel, Paula Fomby, and Kelly Musick. "Siblings and Children's Time Use in the United States." *Demographic Research* 37 (November 28, 2017): 1611–1624. https://doi.org/10.4054/DemRes .2017.37.49.

Thus, siblings also impact how we communicate, deal with conflict, and attach to others.

Most studies looking at family dynamics focus on the parents. Mom, Dad, and other family members who acted as caregivers have a significant influence on our attachment style.* How they raise us can be a lesson in how we react to people in authority. But overlooked in the literature is the influence that siblings have on us. That is why exploring our relationship with them can help us understand why we have an easy or challenging time forming bonds in nonromantic and platonic relationships.

Siblings also uphold healthy and unhealthy generational patterns. As our first friends, they can either encourage or disappoint us. "Siblinghood," which I define as the solidarity of people who are peers linked to a shared cause, interest, concern, condition, or experience, can be far more difficult to achieve if you've had a difficult time connecting with your siblings of origin. Community building relies on people who can get along with their peers and resolve conflict in healthy ways. It can be hard for you to enter spaces and engage in social causes if you're activated by the same behavior that you dislike in your siblings. One way to lessen your fragility when working with people advocating for social justice is to examine the earliest friendships you had right in your household.

Before continuing, I want to address two things. One is the definition of siblings. In the traditional sense, siblings are defined as two or more people having one or both parents as a common ancestor. This, however, does not encompass the wide range of sibling relationships. Siblings can also be foster, chosen, bonus, step, adopted, donor, in-laws, or cousins of similar ages who were raised together. Acknowledging all these configurations is one way to expand our understanding of sibling relationships.

If you're an only child, you can still explore sibling dynamics. This is the second thing I want to address. Perhaps you have a friend or cousin who you consider your best friend and to whom you have been close since childhood. Or, if you grew up as an only child who now parents multiple children, you can look at the ways they relate to each other. People who were not raised with siblings or cousins of the same age may have a romanticized view of sibling relationships. One patron, an only child, shared that she often dreams of what life would be like if she had a sibling. While one study found that only children do not experience adverse psychological or emotional effects being raised

---

* For more on attachment styles, see the work of Dr. John Bowlby.

alone compared to those who were raised with siblings,* it's still important that an only child examines their idealization of siblinghood. Visualizing sibling relationships as perfect and wonderful may create unrealistic expectations when forming bonds with others.

Patrons and workshop attendees who worked through this prompt reported a myriad of emotions when examining their sibling relationships. Many identified that they often took care of their siblings given the environment in which they were raised. When a child takes on a parenting role, this is known as "parentification." It is defined as "children [who] are assigned the role of an adult, taking on both emotional and functional responsibilities that typically are performed by the parent. The parent, in turn, takes the dependent position of the child in the parent-child relationship."** While this definition is often accurate in cases of parents who may be narcissistic or emotionally wounded, compassion should be extended to those where structural barriers created parentification in the home. For example, a single mother working long hours to support her children, or a working two-parent poor family where both parents are hustling to put food on the table and afford rent, show that it's not the parents' *fault* per se that older siblings may suffer parentification. Class issues and a lack of extended family support due to relocation, estrangement, illness, or death are important to consider, and wounds can be formed even when our parents were doing their best.

While some adult duties assigned to a child, such as household chores, are necessary for their healthy development, children who parent their siblings often end up becoming perpetual caregivers as they get older. As adults, they tend to overgive and have a lack of boundaries (you explored this on Day 18). They may also have trouble developing healthy relationships with others. Parentification also tends to be higher in BIPOC*** communities compared to white ones.**** This is yet another reason to consider the entire system, as

---

* Wikle, Jocelyn, Elizabeth Ackert, and Alexander Jensen. "Companionship Patterns and Emotional States During Social Interactions for Adolescents with and Without Siblings." *Journal of Youth and Adolescence* 48 (November 1, 2019). https://doi.org/10.1007/s10964-019-01121-z.

** Engelhardt, Jennifer A. "The Developmental Implications of Parentification: Effects on Childhood Attachment." (2013).

*** An acronym for Black, Indigenous, and People of Color.

**** Preciado, Bertha. "Developmental Implications of Parentification: An Examination of Ethnic Variation and Loneliness." Electronic Theses, Projects, and Dissertations. (2020): 1087. https://scholarworks.lib.csusb.edu/etd/1087.

mentioned above, in which parentification can occur, as it is more likely to occur in families where the parents are under-resourced.

Parentification does not only happen in families with siblings who share DNA. If you had lots of cousins the same age as you, were part of a blended family with bonus or stepsiblings, or bounced around from foster home to foster home, parentification can happen in these family configurations as well. To survive and thrive, a child will play the role of a parent. Another self-preservation tactic within sibling dynamics is estrangement. One workshop attendee shared that she has not had any contact with her siblings in several years. One sibling is an addict; the other is a narcissist. For her safety and mental wellness, she doesn't contact either of them and has chosen not to disclose where she lives.

It's important to keep yourself safe. Your security is more important than putting up with unhealthy behaviors from siblings. In some sibling relation-ships, there is resentment because one gets more attention from their parents than the other. This was the case with de Havilland and Fontaine, the sisters mentioned in the introduction to this chapter. Fontaine battled with many illnesses when she was younger. As a result, her mother's attention was often consumed with Fontaine's health. A sibling who is chronically ill or has a dis-ability can cause the non-ill or nondisabled sibling to feel anger, sadness, and even contempt.* Several patrons and workshop attendees said that, although they love their sibling dearly, they felt hostility towards them due to how much time their parents spent focused on their care.

If resentment was present in your relationship with your sibling(s), this could explain the pangs of jealousy you may feel when one of your "sibs" in the human race needs more attention than you. This is part of the scarcity mentality that you may have suffered as a child, where if one person's needs were attended to, it meant your own were not. Some Historically Undesired Groups (HUGs) may not support other HUGs due to the underlying belief that there is only so much energy or even so much equality to go around. If another group attains their goals, it will somehow usurp the goals of other HUGs, when in fact the opposite is true.

---

* Mitchell, Amy E., Alina Morawska, Raine Vickers-Jones, and Kathryn Bruce. "A Systematic Review of Parenting Interventions to Support Siblings of Children with a Chronic Health Condition." *Clinical Child and Family Psychology Review* 24, no. 3 (September 2021): 651–667. https://doi.org/10.1007/s10567-021-00357-1.

In this social media age, we are made aware of the vast number of global issues that exist. #BlackLivesMatter, #StopAsianHate, #LandBack, #IdleNoMore, #MeToo, #WomensMarch, #ArabSpring, #SOSBlakAustralia, #ShowUpForShabbat, and #UmbrellaRevolution are just some of the hashtags created to bring attention to social justice and human rights issues within a specific community. Names of individuals who have lost their lives due to a social injustice become hashtags as well.[*] When an issue is first raised, there is often an immense amount of support. However, as time goes on, support frequently wanes and animosity towards that community grows, not only among Historically Desired Groups (HDGs) that may perceive the group as threatening their power base, but also among other HUGs who fear that another group is getting all the attention.[**]

Social movements need social relationships that are healthy.[***] You cannot try to dismantle systemic oppression all by yourself. Community actions are what spark change, but if you had problems with your siblings, those same problems can be a trigger when interacting with others. Idolizing sibling relationships can create an expectation that all relationships will be pleasant and peaceful. Disagreements will happen. But instead of walking away and "canceling" someone due to hurt feelings or a difference in opinion, you'll instead handle it in a healthy way.

What Is Possible When You Release Toxic Sibling Dynamics

Authentic friendships can be built. If you have a history of abandoning relationships, disbelieving people's lived experiences, having weak boundaries, and giving too much of yourself too soon, some of these patterns were learned

---

[*] I'm purposely not including the many names that have become hashtags so that I don't exclude anyone because, sadly, the list is too long.

[**] "Racial resentment" is another term used to describe the rise in jealousy directed towards racial communities seeking justice. Read Emmitt Y. Riley and Clarissa Peterson's journal article entitled "I Can't Breathe: Assessing the Role of Racial Resentment and Racial Prejudice in Whites' Feelings Toward Black Lives Matter" in the *National Review of Black Politics* for more on this phenomenon.

[***] Social anxiety may cause some to avoid social interactions due to feelings of being scrutinized, observed, or rejected. Consult with a mental health professional if avoiding social situations is interfering with normal day-to-day activities.

from how you interact with your siblings. One way to show up bravely and consistently for causes you believe in is to address some of these patterns. Although you did not have control over your early conditioning, you do have control over the choices you make today.

Guided Self-Reflective Activities

Step 1—Identify your mood before starting. Go to page 239 and use the Mood Tracker to capture how you're feeling.

Step 2—Nondominant Hand (15 minutes).

Supplies needed: Colored markers or pens, timer.

What to do:

- Set your timer to count down from 15 minutes.
- With your pen, marker, crayon, or other writing instrument, draw or doodle anything you like with your nondominant hand.
- Continue drawing or doodling with your nondominant hand until the timer goes off.

**Use the space below to draw or doodle
with your nondominant hand.**

Step 3—Journal (15 minutes).

Supplies needed: Sketchbook or journal, pen/pencil OR keyboard and screen, timer.

What to do:

- Navigate the prompt using GPS (see page 237).
- Set your timer to count down from 15 minutes.
- Capture the ramblings of your Inner Oppressor in your journal or sketchbook using the following prompts as a guide:

Prompt #1: What sensations or emotions emerged while drawing or doodling with your nondominant hand? What does this tell you about how you handle challenges within platonic, nonromantic relationships?

Prompt #2: What mistakes do you observe in the drawing? How can you accept the messiness with compassion? In what ways can you extend compassion to those who make mistakes in your friendships?

Prompt #3: If you have a romanticized or idealistic view of sibling relationships, what needs to change?

Step 4—Track your mood after completing the Guided Self-Reflective Activities. Go to page 239 and use the Mood Tracker to capture how you're feeling now that you're done.

Congratulations!

You have completed today's actions. Please resist the urge to move quickly to the next day's actions. If you have capacity, you can also file your Summary Report at https://summary.innerfieldtrip.com (optional). Otherwise, go to page 243 and color in the day that you completed on the Journey Tracker page, put the Inner Field Trip aside, get on with your day, then resume tomorrow at the time you booked to meet with your Inner Oppressor.

Explore the Rhythm of the Seasons

In the online community I host called the Inner Field Trip Basecamp (IFTB), cohorts called mini-quests are held around the equinoxes in March and September, and the solstices in June and December. Doing a mini-quest during the equinoxes and solstices made sense because with the changing seasons comes a desire to release old habits and adopt new ones.

It might seem strange that after meeting your Inner Oppressor and exploring perfection, rugged individualism, anti-Blackness, urgency, harshness, body insecurity, people pleasing, appropriation, weaponized kindness, imposter syndrome, and sibling dynamics that you'll now end Part 2 of the 30-day quest looking at the seasons. However, if you're trying to become a better ancestor, tuning into the rhythm of the seasons is a way to be aware of the lessons that nature has for you—something all of our ancestors, regardless of your culture of origin, were more attuned to than we are in contemporary life.

It can be difficult to tune into the natural rhythms of the season if you and your ancestors are not indigenous to the lands you live on. Involuntary and voluntary migration can create a disconnect from the lands. Newly arrived people, whether that arrival was yesterday or a couple centuries ago, are too busy focusing on economic, emotional, and personal recovery. Another reason we disconnect from the lessons the seasons hold is due to overconsumption. As humans, we are consuming too much, putting a strain on our climate, environment, and ecology. The personalities of autumn, winter, summer, and spring are changing due to a planet, in the words of Outkast, that is "dying and crying because of [our actions].""

Due to the effects of colonialism, a colonized mind socialized in a colonized way can only imagine a future that's colonized. Thus, one way to build a deep respect for the lands you live on is to prioritize Indigenous wisdom. People who have lived on the lands for millennia hold knowledge that settlers and their descendants do not. We would do well to listen to water, land, and environmental defenders because they are fiercely protecting nature so that those who come after us have lands to live on. Conservation efforts are incomplete if Indigenous people and nations are not consulted.

As we continue to build our respect for Indigenous wisdom, tuning into the seasons is another way to grow our care for the earth. Nature isn't "on" all the time. It goes through periods of rest and renewal. The sun will always rise and set. When it disappears from the sky, the moon and stars make their appearance. The sun isn't competing against the moon for which can be the brightest. You don't see a cosmic battle taking place in the skies as the sun and moon jockey for position. Each has its time in the sky and shares it equally (as with the equinoxes) or not (as with the solstices).

What a beautiful lesson the sun, moon, and stars teach us about the principle of abundance. There is more than enough for you and me. Sometimes, you will shine brightly. Other times, I will. Just because the focus is on me doesn't mean that you're unimportant. Within activism, some causes will be prioritized; others will not. As I said on Day 12 about anti-Blackness, focus does not mean exclusion. Concentrating on Black lives does not mean that other people are not important. Tuning into the rhythm of the solstices and equinoxes and how the sun and moon make room for each other would help lessen the need for "whataboutism."

The dance of the sun and moon is a part of seasonal changes. So, too, are the various seasons of the year. In countries that are quite a distance from the equator, there are four distinct seasons—autumn, winter, spring, and summer. For countries closer to the equator or the poles, there seems to be just one season. However, even in single-season countries, there are variations in conditions. For example, in countries near the equator, it's hot all the time. However, in the winter months, it's hot and rainy while in the summer months,

---

* Outkast. "Da Art of Storytellin', Part 2," track 10 on *Aquemini* (Arista Records, 1998, Apple Music).

it's hot and dry. In countries near the poles, the sun doesn't rise for many weeks during the winter months whereas, in the summer, the sun doesn't set for days. Even though I'm going to refer to four distinct seasons in the rest of this chapter, you can still learn valuable information even if you live in a single-season country. Just adjust as you read along.

Summer is the first season that we'll explore. Some anticipate the arrival of summer. The warm sun, longer days, and relaxed schedules excite summer lovers. They get to slow down, enjoy the weather, and spend more time with friends and family members. Mae, a patron who lives in Canada, said this of summer:

> This prompt made me very aware of my relationship with summer's fleeting sensual pleasures, the flavors of homegrown fruit and vegetables, the burn of sunshine on my skin, the shock of slipping under cool water, crisp sand underfoot, bright colored flowers in my garden, the sound of cicadas everywhere. If I can't get myself to the beach in summer, I feel I've "wasted" the season. I feel resentful whenever obligation calls me away from summer's hedonism.

There are others, however, who detest the summer months. The warm sun represents stifling heat and sticky humidity. The longer days contribute to noise pollution from people spending copious amounts of time outdoors. Patrons from Historically Undesired Groups (HUGs) who did this prompt became aware of generational memories, which was at the root of their dislike of summer. One in particular, a Black Latin woman, found a connection between her loathing of summer and what her ancestors had to endure working on sugarcane plantations in Latin America. She never worked under the searing heat of the sun with no pay or rest, yet she was embodying a generational memory in her reflections about summer.

Relaxed schedules mean that predictable routines cease to exist. For some, summer represents boredom, anxiety, and irritation. Due to structural barriers, such as disability, poverty, or migration status, some are not able to relax over the summer months. One patron, a child of immigrant parents, could not participate in conversations their classmates were having about planned getaways and faraway trips. They had to stay inside a hot apartment with no air-conditioning. Their parents could not afford to pay for summer camps or vacations and couldn't take time off since they had to work. Summer, to this person, meant isolation and solitude.

Summer teaches us to slow down and enjoy the pleasures that come with gathering with others and being outdoors, but if we have not had those experiences, we may need to create rituals in our lives that help us reclaim the lessons of summer. Even if we do not have the luxury of working less during the summer, or if excessive heat is difficult due to outdoor labor or lack of cool environments, we can still do our best to schedule time to tune in to the lessons of summer, whether it is a trip to the beach on a weekend or just going for a walk each day after work to feel the summer breeze on our skin. Free city pools, urban gardens, and bike rides along a river are all ways that you can create a "summer break" vibe in pockets of our lives, even though you are no longer a child who enjoys a long summer break from school.

Fall, on the other hand, has a different personality than summer. Schedules become predictable, people stop barbecuing and socializing outdoors, and there's a return to the busyness of school and work. To some, the shortened days bring a sense of peace and quiet. The sounds and smells that noisily crept through the window during summertime have become muted. The irritation of the hot sun transforms into a welcome cooling of the days.

Fall is a time of harvest, preparation, reflection, and letting go. Whatever was planted is now ready to be picked. Whatever was picked is now ready to be stored away. The leaves falling to the ground will need to be swept up and discarded. Patrons and workshop attendees who did this prompt reported that fall feels like a fresh start. Just like the trees shedding their leaves, some use fall to get rid of old conditioning to make way for new ways of thinking.

Letting go of old ways of thinking, similar to how trees let go of their leaves, is one thing some associate with autumn. The fall equinox is a time when light and dark are equal, prompting some to seek balance. For others, fall represents sadness about getting back to overpacked schedules. Rue shared a memory about her grandmother as she reflected on fall:

The connections between the dominant culture's notions of being hyper-productive and perfect are very much entwined with how I think about this time of year. Fall brings up a lot of sadness and reminds me of how I've so often felt out of place or out of rhythm with the rest of life, the rest of society. I've only recently learned how to relax and enjoy unstructured time which summer represents. Going into fall feels off in a way. It's probably because this time of year makes me think of my grandmother who embodied fall to me. She was steady, reliable, and exemplary, traits I failed to appreciate when she was alive. I got a good cry from having the chance to see her love in a new light.

The spiritual significance of fall teaches us that we, too, need to reap the fruits of our labor, let go of that which no longer serves us, and rid our space, energy, and emotions of what needs to be discarded, plus reflect on what we should preserve and keep. While fall is often thought of as a season in which flowers die and leaves fall, it's important to appreciate the bright splendor of leaves changing colors, then falling to the ground. Fall is a season of renewal.

As people trade in pumpkin spice lattes for candy cane ones, the transition from fall to winter evokes strong emotions, as out of all the seasons, winter is the one that is disliked the most. Some complain bitterly about the cold and lack of sunlight. Some equate winter to a kind of sustained blankness and death. The trees are barren, the birds disappear, and the gray palette that overpowers nature is bleak and sad. Winter, however, is misunderstood. There is a spiritual significance of winter. The cold, barren landscape still has life stirring underneath the snow and hardened ground. Liora, a patron, has fond memories of winter regarding Hanukkah:

I really enjoyed the fact that this year Hanukkah happened in early December. It is different each year. This year it was quiet and meditative for our family. Eva (my spouse) lit candles. We then sat and watched TV together and talked until the candles burned down. We had more time together than usual in the evening. I did go to a Hanukkah party at a local synagogue that is very inclusive in many ways and social justice oriented. The lights of many menorahs were beautiful and I felt hopeful.

Yes, the trees are barren, the vegetation is buried under blankets of snow, and birds and insects disappear. Nothing moves except the bitterly cold wind through the leave-less branches. However, under the stillness is vitality. The trees are barren, but the roots are still alive. Insects and small animals are not visible, but they're moving around under the fluffy snow and packed soil. What appears like death is anything but. Winter is all about serenity and patience.

To embrace winter is to welcome reflection, contemplation, and introspection. Withdrawing from interactions and removing distractions is a great way to achieve clarity. The long nights are an invitation to explore the deep crevices of your shadow, the place where your unconscious biases hide. Some embrace the invitation that winter extends to reflect, and yet to do so can be an advantage that others are not able to enjoy, as Bev explains:

> My Inner Oppressors tell me that withdrawing and hibernating during my personal winter is a privilege. It tells me I have to perform my activism so others know that I care. Stillness, however, helps me get clear. Withdrawing can help me concentrate on what my purpose is. Withdrawing could help me restore my depleted energy and develop trust in myself that I can do what I need for myself to live out my purpose.

There is a difference between hibernating and hiding. When animals hibernate during the winter, they do so to conserve energy during a time of year when resources are scarce. For humans, hibernation takes the form of withdrawing from social, personal, and professional obligations when your emotional, psychological, financial, and physical resources are low. Hiding is when you ghost, disappear, or vanish due to fear or feeling unsafe. Knowing the difference can help you understand, like Bev, why embracing a personal winter is a source of self-preservation.

Winter is also an invitation to spend time with those you love. Celebrating rituals with others, as Liora does with her wife, Eva, are ways that some add warmth to the coldness of the season. However, the excessive social demands, and not the overpowering darkness and cold, can create gloom for some. Leanne made this clear after reflecting on winter:

> Buying presents, attending holiday parties, and meeting multiple external deadlines exhaust me, especially in the days leading up to Christmas. Not only do the social demands make me tired, but so do the bright lights, loud holiday music, and excessive cheer. It makes me sound like a Scrooge at this time of year, but now I understand why he lived alone!

Winter isn't a sign of death; it's a sign of rest. Our culture, however, does not prioritize rest, and so it is that we busy ourselves with excessive consumption—which can tax and stress us out both economically and in terms of our time—fearing that our holiday presents won't be "good enough" and forcing us into frequent contact with our families of origin for holiday festivities, even when that may bring up old issues and anxiety for us. Slowing down and putting limits on the commercialization of the season, reclaiming how and what we celebrate and with whom, and honoring our inner rhythms brought on by the shortened days are ways we can tap into the restfulness of winter.

As the freezing days turn into cool ones, winter gives way to spring. Spring is a time of year to get rid of all that no longer serves you. That is where the term "spring cleaning" comes from. The snow melts and reveals all the debris it's been covering. This inspires a need to clean out what is toxic and dirty. Spring is also a season of new beginnings. The buds grow, flowers bloom, and birds chirp—all signaling a period of fertility, growth, and rebirth. Cate Moon, a patron, embraces spring with all its newness:

> As I move into spring, the beliefs that I am letting go of—the beliefs that I'm not enough, that I don't matter, that I need to take care of others, or that I need a man—are all beliefs handed to me by the dominant culture. The idea of blooming is so exciting to me moving into my personal spring.

Spring teaches us that we, too, need to allow things to grow in our life. Whatever needs to be discarded after emerging from your personal winter will help you make space for rebirth and growth during spring.

What Is Possible When You Tune into the Rhythm of the Seasons

Periods of rest and productivity are a human right. You are not a machine. You cannot work seven days a week for 20 hours a day for the rest of your life. With all their splendor and glory, the changing seasons teach you that after periods of immense activity, there are periods of rest and rejuvenation. As the Nap Bishop, Tricia Hersey, declares in her book, *Rest Is Resistance: A Manifesto.* What you resist is the pressure to be out of alignment with the rhythms of nature by being "on" all the time.

Interconnectedness deepens between humans and nature. Your Inner Oppressor works in tandem with the dominant culture to train you into believing that you are all alone. By tuning into the rhythm of the seasons, you are reminded that if you care for nature, it will care for you. Having clean air to breathe, solid ground to walk on, and clean water to drink are not privileges to be earned. As an environmental steward, you are obligated to change your consumption behaviors so you leave the earth better than you found it.

Environmental justice grows for others. The rhythm of the seasons broadens your viewpoint on climate issues and environmental justice. Some do not have clean water or air due to the actions of those who abuse their advantages. As you see a connection between your right to a clean environment, you can't help but be in solidarity with those who are seeking environmental justice.

Guided Self-Reflective Activities

Step 1—Identify your mood before starting. Go to page 239 and use the Mood Tracker to capture how you're feeling.

Step 2—Seasonal Doodle (15 minutes).

	**Supplies needed:** Colored markers or pens, timer.
	What to do: ✂ Set your timer to count down from 15 minutes. ✂ Reflect on the season you like the least. ✂ Draw or doodle images associated with the season you like the least. Use colors associated with that season to bring your drawings or doodles to life.

Use the space below to doodle images associated
with the season you like the least.

Step 3—Journal (15 minutes).

Supplies needed: Sketchbook or journal, pen/pencil OR keyboard and screen, timer.

What to do:

- Navigate the prompt using GPS (see page 237).
- Set your timer to count down from 15 minutes.
- Capture the ramblings of your Inner Oppressor in your journal or sketchbook using the following prompts as a guide:

Prompt #1: What lessons can you learn from the season that you like the least? What memories do you need to heal? What new story do you need to tell? What forgiveness do you need to extend to yourself?

Prompt #2: How would your life look differently if you were more in tune with the rhythms of the seasons? What needs to change? What are you already doing well?

Prompt #3: Which areas of your life feel out of balance? Which season can you model to help bring clarity and a possible solution?

Step 4—Track your mood after completing the Guided Self-Reflective Activities. Go to page 239 and use the Mood Tracker to capture how you're feeling now that you're done.

Congratulations!

You have completed today's actions. Please resist the urge to move quickly to the next day's actions. If you have capacity, you can also file your Summary Report at https://summary.innerfieldtrip.com (optional). Otherwise, go to page 243 and color in the day that you completed on the Journey Tracker page, put the Inner Field Trip aside, get on with your day, then resume tomorrow at the time you booked to meet with your Inner Oppressor.

Active Rest Stop

Once again, you have reached another Active Rest Stop, and they are built into the 30-day Inner Field Trip quest so that you take a moment to pause. You have encountered one on Day 11, 15, 20, and the last one today on Day 25. To remind yourself why we take a moment to pause during the Inner Field Trip, go back and review Day 11.

What to Do During an Active Rest Stop

As a reminder, instead of reviewing the art or writings you produced during the previous three or four days, you will instead focus on creating, building, composing, moving, or making. Resmaa Menakem recommends discharging and dispersing energy nurtured through conflict or high-stress situations using movement, such as dance, playing sports, exercise, or physical labor.[*] Movement is encouraged during the Active Rest Stop, and so, too, are creative and artistic pursuits. The infographic on the following page gives some ideas on what you can do during the Active Rest Stop.

The font may be a bit small, so I've listed the six categories and related activities below:

- **Build It**—Building Blocks, Popsicle Sticks, Toothpicks, Glue Gun, Model Toy, Jigsaw Puzzle, Slime, Play-Doh, Mimetic Sand

- **Make It**—Knitting, Sewing, Crocheting, Needlepoint, Embroidery, Beading, Woodworking, Baking

---

[*] Menakem, Resmaa. *My Grandmother's Hands: Racialized Trauma and the Pathway to Mending Our Hearts and Bodies* (Las Vegas: Central Recovery Press, 2017), Chapter 12.

ACTIVE REST STOP IDEAS

- **Illustrate It**—Painting, Drawing, Cartooning, Collaging, Junk Journaling, Diamond Painting, Lettering

- **Compose / Write It**—Music, Screenplay, Memoir, Pandemic Reflections, Creative Writing, TV Script, One-Person Show, Play, Poetry

- **Move It**—Walking, Hiking, Dancing, Cycling, Trampolining, Skating, Exercising

- **Reflect on It**—Meditating, Praying, Napping, Deep Breathing, Listening to Calm Music, Yoga, Bubble Bathing, Playing Calm Music on an Instrument

Some things to remember when engaging in an Active Rest Stop:

- You're not doing this to be seen, published, or applauded. In other words, let go of any expectation of what your creation could become. Just be in the creating mood.

- It's best to do the activity solo, but if you want to include someone, choose someone with the most childlike personality. You don't want to do this with someone who's going to descend into criticism or complaints (whether directed at you or themselves).

- The activity you choose for the Active Rest Stop can be the same one you do during the next one, or totally different.

- Set the timer for 30 minutes and then let your creativity take over. Color outside the lines. Leave the mess on the floor. Play a wrong note. Write using run-on sentences. Use your nondominant hand to paint. Create a Play-Doh tree with red bark and purple leaves. Enjoy the messiness of the activity and release perfection.

Active Rest Stop Activities

Step 1—Identify your mood before starting. Go to page 239 and use the Mood Tracker Ring to capture how you're feeling.

Step 2—Engage in the Active Rest Stop (30 minutes).

	Supplies needed: Materials to engage in the Active Rest Stop, timer.
	What to do: - Choose one Active Rest Stop activity. - Take a few minutes to set up your play or studio space. - Start the timer, then engage in the activity until the timer goes off.

Step 3—Fill in the blanks. Once the timer goes off and before tidying up your play or studio space, complete the sentences below. Spend no more than 15 seconds on each question, and jot down some thoughts.

After engaging in the Active Rest Stop, my Inner Oppressor revealed:

_____

_____

_____

_____

It's no wonder because:

_____

_____

_____

_____

Therefore, the one action I will take is:

_____

_____

_____

_____

Step 4—Track your mood after completing the Guided Self-Reflective Activities. Go to page 239 and use the Mood Tracker Ring to capture how you're feeling now that you're done.

Congratulations!

You have completed today's actions. Please resist the urge to move quickly to the next day's actions. If you have capacity, you can also file your Summary Report at https://summary.innerfieldtrip.com (optional). Otherwise, go to page 243 and color in the day that you completed on the Journey Tracker page, put the Inner Field Trip aside, get on with your day, then resume tomorrow at the time you booked to meet with your Inner Oppressor.

PART

3

After the Quest

Protecting the Work You've Done

When I'm within sight of the parking lot after hiking for hours, I get impatient. I can't wait to get to my car, take off my heavy backpack, and lean against my vehicle. My feet are tired, my muscles are aching, and depending on the weather, I want to either warm up with the heater turned on or cool off with the air-conditioning on full blast.

It's during these last 10–20 minutes of my hours-long hike that I have to be very careful. Because I'm distracted by what awaits me when I get to the trailhead, I don't pick up my feet high enough. As a result, there's a higher chance that I may trip and fall on the rugged trail. Although I'm eager to end my hike, I'm also aware that I need to pay attention to any hazards along the way. I have to focus on each step; otherwise I could injure myself.

This is the same for the Inner Field Trip. You have completed 25 grueling days of marching through your interior to meet your Inner Oppressor and find out why it acts the way it does. You have used guided art and journaling prompts, collectively known as Guided Self-Reflective Activities, to identify perfection, rugged individualism, anti-Blackness, anti-Indigeneity, anti-Semitism, and other forms of ethnic and ethno-religious stereotyping, urgency, harshness, body insecurity, appropriation, weaponized kindness, imposter syndrome, and your relationship to capitalism, nature, pleasure, rest, and productivity. You have experienced just about every emotion and allowed your body to recall just about every sensation. After going on this solo inner trek, you may want to sprint to the end so you can end this quest.

There are, however, some hazards along the way as you march towards the end. How you handle these hazards will be the difference between being the first in your lineage to pass on healing or continuing the long tradition of transmitting pain. The last five days of the Inner Field Trip quest, Days 26–30, will help you protect what you've done. Otherwise, you won't be prepared for the various factors that can sabotage your Inner Field Trip experience.

Please proceed to Day 26 to start the process of building your resilience and courage as you return to a culture that has not changed.

The Discomfort You're Feeling Is . . .

I used to host the 30-day Inner Field Trip as a 10-day quest inside my online community every quarter. On the last day, I'd invite patrons to design a plan of action, asking how they'll use their newfound discoveries to become a more authentic activist. Instead of a timeline of who they'll contact, what they'll do, and by when, I, instead, got pushback. Some delayed the creation of the action plan due to exhaustion. Others said they were confused by what I was asking them to do, despite my very clear instructions. Some frankly disappeared.

I noticed the same reactions when I hosted the Inner Field Trip experience in workshop rooms. Instead of excitement and eagerness after completing the Guided Self-Reflective Activities and meeting with their Inner Oppressor, attendees displayed some of the same emotions as patrons—sadness, confusion, indifference, denial, numbness, guilt, and anger. The one thing that wasn't obvious with my patrons that was visible with workshop attendees was how their bodies were responding. I could not see my patrons when they worked through the activities as they were virtual. However, the somatic cues were obvious with workshop attendees. Tear-streaked faces, trembling voices, excessive coughing, downcast eyes, and slumped shoulders were just some of the visible cues that became clear while in the room with attendees.

I became curious about what I was witnessing. The emotional, behavioral, and somatic reactions occurring after doing the hardest part of the Inner Field Trip needed to be named, acknowledged, and cared for. It wasn't until I read two resources, a book entitled *The Racial Healing Handbook* by Anneliese A. Singh and a workbook entitled *Decolonize First* by Ta7talíya Michelle Lorna

Nahanee, that I could finally name what I was observing. Singh and Nahanee identified that grief is what emerges after going through a process of deep introspection.

You may think that grief and mourning are only experienced by those who have lost a loved one; however, grief and mourning relate to any type of loss. During the COVID-19 pandemic, some were grieving the loss of plans, income, stability, and safety, in addition to mourning the loss of loved ones due to the virus. When humans attach value to something or someone and that person, place, or thing disappears, there is a sense of deep emotional pain.

After going through Days 8–25 of the Inner Field Trip, you may be feeling hopeless, helpless, aimless, or worthless. When you started the quest, you had some sense of who you are, what you want to do, and where you want to end up. However, as you interrogated your Inner Oppressor about the ways you've been complicit in upholding systems of oppression, the loss of identity, purpose, and belonging can be too great a burden.

As was indicated on Day 19, appropriation is a tool someone uses when they're without culture. Now that you've explored your unconscious biases, you're aware now more than ever that you just cannot align with the dominant culture any longer. In this case, you are a cultural exile, a person with no sense of belonging. You no longer want to hold membership in the dominant culture; however, you're not sure which culture you should belong to.

Historically Undesired Groups (HUGs), on the other hand, have felt like cultural exiles for generations. Laws and legislation were drafted to prevent those whose ancestors were colonized from participating in their customs, speaking their languages, and performing their rituals. Forced migration, genocide, and political and economic instability caused by imperialism disconnected HUGs from their lands and removed their knowledge keepers. HUGs have tried to adapt to the dominant culture but have always been made to feel like outsiders. If you identify with HUGs, you've been feeling as if, no matter what you do, you cannot adapt to the dominant culture and your culture of origin is now foreign to you.

What unites Historically Desired Groups (HDGs) and HUGs at this point in the Inner Field Trip experience is a shared feeling of cultural alienation. One of my former co-facilitators, an African American woman, said to a room full of workshop attendees that, now, HDGs understand the feeling of identitylessness, something she and her ancestors have felt for centuries. This wasn't, however, an insult or a way to get back at HDGs. In other words, my former co-facilitator wasn't saying, "Good. Now you know how wandering feels because my ancestors and I have been doing it for centuries." Instead, my former co-facilitator used this analogy as an invitation for HDGs to join HUGs in creating a new culture.

Before you can create a new, human-centered culture, you must be aware that you're in a very tender stage in your Inner Field Trip quest. Feeling aimless, purposeless, and identityless can cause you to return to what you know. The temptation will be great as you see others living their best life as clueless participants within the dominant culture. You may miss the fellowship, fidelity, and friendship when you were in a state of utter bliss and innocence. At a workshop that I hosted in Portland, Oregon, an attendee shared that they were unable to attend family gatherings and stay quiet when a problematic family member says something harmful. At the same time, this attendee also acknowledged that to confront that family member meant that they would no longer be invited to family gatherings ever again. This realization brought them into a state of sorrow.

This in-between stage can be quite uncomfortable. You want to return to familiarity, but you don't want to dismantle the work you've done so far. If you classify this stage as a feeling of emptiness, you will be vulnerable to the seductive playlist of the dominant culture. Emptiness is equal to isolation and loneliness. In Buddhism, emptiness is a state that one wants to achieve because it means that you've emptied yourself of all the clutter so that you can meet your higher self. It is an ideal state of being. In the Inner Field Trip framework, emptiness indicates the void that one feels as a cultural exile. Emptiness is a feeling of voidness and an undesired state that produces loneliness, aimlessness, and purposelessness.

If, instead, you see the liminal space—the in-between—as a process of emptying, this will protect you from returning to the dominant culture. When in a state of emptying, you are continuing the process of ridding yourself of the toxic beliefs and the unconscious biases that prevented you from tuning into your true self. Your purpose when emptying is to continue the process of emptying. This, along with the goals you stated in Day 2, are what you and your Inner Oppressor should cling to as you embrace emptying and not emptiness. Asha Frost, Indigenous Medicine Woman and author of *You Are the Medicine*, states that emptying is medicine, something that is meant to heal you:

I have gone through this same experience enough to know that if I honor this season with love, I will come out on the other side with beautiful new seeds to plant and ideas to co-create. While I am still learning to love the void, at least now I can trust that this season doesn't last forever.[*]

In the next chapter, you will make some commitments. These are the beautiful new seeds that you will plant. Before doing so, you need to reflect on your losses. This is an important step because if you don't hold space for what you and your Inner Oppressor are grieving, you'll never be able to become a better ancestor. The shock, denial, anger, bargaining, depression, testing, and acceptance, also known as the stages of grief, need to be witnessed, processed, and embraced.[**] Your Inner Oppressor has a new role to play as it continues to keep you safe within systems of oppression. You are also adapting to a new role now that your unconscious biases are conscious.

One clue as to which feeling has been the strongest while going on an Inner Field Trip is to review the Mood Tracker. Although there are still a few days left in the 30-day quest, you can start the evaluation process now. Looking at the Mood Tracker can help you get clear on which emotion or feeling was activated the most while you were engaging in Days 1–25.

For this Grief Debrief, there is no need to review the self-reflective art or writings you did between Days 8–25. In fact, I discourage you from doing so. First, you may become overwhelmed by the sheer amount of data. Second, you may self-oppress or self-injure while reviewing what you drew or wrote. Reading your Inner Oppressor's angry, sad, or confusing words may cause you to do whatever it takes to make yourself look good, superior, or exceptional—the very traits you've worked so hard to identify and release. This may then lead to the third reason why you should not review what you drew or wrote, as you may want to satisfy your perfectionism and edit or modify what you did. Instead, follow the steps on the next page to evaluate your mood and complete the Grief Debrief.

---

[*] Frost, Asha. *You Are the Medicine: 13 Moons of Indigenous Wisdom, Ancestral Connection, and Animal Spirit Guidance* (New York: Hay House, 2022), 38.

[**] Dr. Elisabeth Kübler-Ross wrote about the stages of grief in her seminal book, *On Death and Dying*. The stages of grief gave the impression that there was a correct way to mourn, moving from one step to the next in a time-limited and linear fashion. Dr. Kübler-Ross expanded the five stages to seven and clarified that the process of grieving is nonlinear, does not have a time limit, and some emotions may not be felt at all or could be felt at the same time.

Guided Self-Reflective Activities

Step 1—Identify your mood before starting. Go to page 239 and use the Mood Tracker to capture how you're feeling.

Step 2—Use the Mood Tracker Ring to document the number of times the mood showed up using the following grids. One or two moods should overshadow the others before and after doing the Guided Self-Reflective Activities.

How many days did you feel the following moods *before* starting the Guided Self-Reflective Activity?

MOOD	Happy	Sad	Unsure	Angry	Tired	Calm
NUMBER OF DAYS						

How many days did you feel the following moods *after* completing the Guided Self-Reflective Activity?

MOOD	Happy	Sad	Unsure	Angry	Tired	Calm
NUMBER OF DAYS						

Before continuing, I want to assure you that the number of days you felt something—whether the number is high or low—does not mean something is wrong with you. In fact, you should be proud that you are doing what most people refuse to do. You are meeting with your Inner Oppressor, exploring generations of unconscious biases so you can become a better ancestor.

Step 3—Journal (15 minutes).

Supplies needed: Journal, pen/pencil OR keyboard and screen, timer.

What to do:

- Navigate the prompt using GPS (see page 237).
- Set your timer to count down from 15 minutes.
- Capture the ramblings of your Inner Oppressor in your journal or sketchbook using the following prompts as a guide:

Prompt #1: Which one to two moods did you feel the most BEFORE starting each day of the quest and AFTER completing it? When you look back at those days of the quest, what about the theme made you feel that way?

Prompt #2: How do you typically express grief when you lose something or someone? What does this tell you about how you are managing grief in this chapter?

Prompt #3: What is your Inner Oppressor mourning the loss of based on what was revealed in the Mood Tracker?

Step 4—Track your mood after completing the Guided Self-Reflective Activities. Go to page 239 and use the Mood Tracker to capture how you're feeling now that you're done.

Congratulations!

You have completed today's actions. Please resist the urge to move quickly to the next day's actions. If you have capacity, you can also file your Summary Report at https://summary.innerfieldtrip.com (optional). Otherwise, go to page 243 and color in the day that you completed on the Journey Tracker page, put the Inner Field Trip aside, get on with your day, then resume tomorrow at the time you booked to meet with your Inner Oppressor.

Update Your MAPS

*T*hose last few steps towards the trailhead can be challenging. As I'm hiking back to the parking lot, I'm thinking about the food I'm going to eat, the shower I'm going to take, and the bruises I'm going to tend to. I'm also replaying the beautiful scenes I've seen during my hike. A pristine waterfall, a crystal-clear river, a noisy wild turkey, even the short conversations I had with other hikers along the trail. I reflect upon the sights and sounds that I enjoyed on my hike, which creates a deep sense of joy while I also become hyperaware of my aches and pains.

On Day 26, you reflected on the losses. Whatever you're grieving the loss of is valid. Within grief, there is also remembrance of the good times and things that went well. This is the nature of grief. You can feel sadness and anger, then feel joy and happiness. Sometimes, you will feel all these emotions at once. Part of reflecting on the losses is also to think about the gains.

It may be difficult to hold space for both loss and joy at the same time. If you're mourning, you may believe that you must remain in a sad, gloomy, and pensive state for a set period. You may even believe that joy is "inappropriate" now that you have grappled with how much is wrong in the world. If you're a member of a Historically Desired Group (HDG), or even a member of a Historically Undesired Group (HUG) who overlaps with HDGs, such as being a white woman, a white man with a disability, or a straight, cis, abled man of color, you may feel that to come away from this journey with "happiness" would make you a callous person who does not care about the suffering of others.

Feeling sad and outraged for the rest of time is how you think you should feel as a show of solidarity with HUGs. This is not the case. One of the best ways to combat systems of oppression is to find a deep inner happiness that exists outside of those systems. As complex human beings, joy and happiness will show up even amid deep pain and regret. Through wars, famines, tragedies, and personal losses, human beings continue to find joy and make meaning, to love and be loved, and to find self-acceptance and peace. This is part of what makes us human and allows us to evolve and change.

I have observed in my work with the Inner Field Trip and in other capacities the tension between joy and grief. Since I was a teenager, I have played the organ at countless church services and funerals. Over the past several decades, I've passively observed the various ways people grieve as I play "Amazing Grace" in F-major for the umpteenth time. I've heard many eulogies and tributes shared about the dearly departed. Some eulogies cause the speaker to break down in tears, unable to finish what they wanted to say. Others cause those who have gathered to burst out in uncontrollable laughter as humorous moments about the dearly departed are shared. Being an organist at many funerals has taught me that we can hold space for all emotions, even during the most somber of occasions.

It is also important to stipulate that feeling happiness and joy does not mean just "forgetting" what you have learned here and going about your life as it was. As you reflect on what your Inner Oppressor revealed, you may find yourself ready to make some new commitments. In her book *Me and White Supremacy*, Layla F. Saad states that commitments allow you to create actions you'll do daily "with the consistent commitment to keep learning, keep showing up, and keep doing what is necessary so that BIPOC (Black, Indigenous, and People of Color) can live with dignity and equality."[*] Looking at what you've gained, or what you're saying yes to, and connecting it back to the type of ancestor you want to become is a good way to stay aligned with your commitments.

Within the Inner Field Trip, the gains that patrons and workshop attendees tend to express are those related to thinking, being, doing, and having. To make this easier to remember, the gains can be thought of as MAPS. A map gives you information about where to go and how to get there. If the map hasn't been updated in quite some time, the outdated information will direct you to the wrong place. The MAPS used in the Inner Field Trip cover four

---

[*] Saad, Laya F., *Me and White Supremacy: Combat Racism, Change the World, and Become a Good Ancestor.* Naperville: Sourcebooks (2020): 200.

specific things people tend to make a commitment to after completing the most grueling part of the Inner Field Trip and before they reach the absolute end of the quest. The four are listed below.

M = METHODS

This refers to a way of doing something, such as habits. Before engaging in the Inner Field Trip, you may have talked over others, shown up in the comments section as a keyboard activist and dismissed the lived experience of a HUG, or laughed along with your buddies as they told racist, homophobic, or sexist jokes. Since your goal is to become a better ancestor (as indicated on Day 2), you need to say yes to new patterns and habits that are pro-human and pro-equity.

Making a commitment to do better can be hard if you have a tough relationship with consistency. For some, being disciplined robs them of their spontaneity. For others, they cling to routines obsessively due to a chaotic upbringing. Systemic issues, such as unemployment and underemployment, insecure housing, and identity-based oppression, can leave some experiencing inconsistency despite their individual efforts. The dominant culture also makes the status quo look comforting and appealing, which may look attractive to you. It's important to understand what can cause you to abandon routines as you make a commitment to creating new ones. Kayla, a patron, observed their renewed sense for creating better habits after working through the roadblocks with their Inner Oppressor:

> Discipline was absent and inconsistent growing up. Lots of confusion and feeling like the concept of discipline itself is beyond me in some ways. Another thing was that the people I hung out with made fun of those with discipline, so I ended up picking up on that, too. I'm glad to have bypassed some roadblocks here so I can keep working at it.

Staying consistent can be difficult, but the good news is that you've gotten this far in the Inner Field Trip. That means that you have it in you to stick with something over a period of time. Use that energy to make daily, weekly, and monthly commitments to prioritize equality and equity. Examples include speaking up when someone says something oppressive, doing research on your ancestry, following a variety of BIPOCs on socials, reading books written

by BIPOCs, learning about a new culture, supporting an organization or political candidate who demonstrates a commitment to equity and inclusion and
is a member of a HUG, supporting BIPOC-owned businesses, or even just fun
activities like learning a new language so as to open yourself up to a new
culture.

A = ATTITUDES

These are the beliefs, values, and worldviews that you hold. Going on the Inner
Field Trip has helped you become aware that innocence, superiority, privilege,
resentment, fragility, silence, intellectualization, complicity, mockery, centering, denial, and exceptionalism are a problem. If you identify with HUGs, the
Inner Field Trip has made you aware of the ways that systems of oppression
have made you feel inferior and less than. Lianne, a patron, shared that she is
making a commitment to curiosity regarding her ancestry:

> I'm viewing the discomfort that I'm feeling right now with a sense of curi-
> osity. I'm asking my Inner Oppressor, "Where will we go? What will we
> learn? What are you trying to tell me?" Curiosity has given me the cour-
> age to explore my ancestry more and to find out where my ancestors
> were from pre-colonization.

In addition to curiosity, some of the other beliefs that patrons and workshop
attendees make commitments to are compassion, cooperation, receptive-
ness, humility, openness, vulnerability, surrender, creativity, spaciousness, rec-
iprocity, community, and choice. Use these as guidelines to prioritize the
attitudes you're committed to embodying.

P = PARTNERSHIPS

This refers to the new associations and connections you'll create. Perhaps
you'll make a commitment to working with causes, charities, organizations,
and community groups (both online and offline) that align with your goal in
becoming a better ancestor instead of trying to be performative. Committing
to a justice-oriented lifestyle can happen best when done in communion with
those who are already doing the work. Some patrons identified that participating in causes with others keeps them motivated. One patron noted that,

as a competitive athlete, she was used to doing things on her own. She won-ders how many relationships she has harmed due to wanting to win and desir-ing to be first. Her aim is to become a relational ancestor, and she understands that, to do so, she needs to temper her ego so she can build healthier part-nerships with those who are already doing the work.

Being in partnership with others is a desire that emerges after interrogating individualism and urgency. This doesn't mean that you can't launch a charity or fundraiser on your own. Instead, you do your research to see if you're better off contributing your advantages to a charity, cause, or community group that is under-resourced financially. You interrogate whether you need to center yourself in those efforts or whether you can support those who are more expe-rienced. These decisions can be made in a variety of ways, such as how much time you can give, whether you have a large platform such that your leader-ship would genuinely help bring new people to support your chosen cause, and the availability of other resources in your area. For example, if you live in a large city, there is probably less need to launch a whole new organization versus finding an existing one that aligns with your passions.

Remember to align your partnerships with the ancestor you identified that you want to become on Day 2. An environmental ancestor would want to form partnerships with conservation groups. An ideological ancestor would work with an organization that preserves art and writings or help underfunded charities trademark their intellectual property. It's important to choose the associations that align with which ancestor you are becoming.

S = SKILLS AND STRENGTHS

What can you do really, really well? I'm not talking about the social, ethnic, biological, or behavioral identities (SEBBIs) that you have inherited due to your nationality, culture, or genetics. I'm referring to the creative, athletic, or artistic aptitudes that you do naturally. These are the innate strengths and talents you were born with. When you can identify your strengths and use them to agitate for change, you'll never get caught up in the guilt of thinking you're not doing activism the right way. You'll stay on the trail that aligns with your unique skill set, as that's what will help you stick with the work long term.

It is far better to use your writing skills to write letters to politicians or use your orator skills to deliver speeches to decision makers if it means you'll do this over and over without getting tired or bored. If you're good with web design, you can volunteer your time to build websites for causes, charities, organizations, and community groups (this can also satisfy the P in MAPS, as this is an example of the partnerships you can form). These small actions that you do each day or week have as much impact in changing systems as do marches, protests, and sit-ins. Choosing forms of activism and advocacy that align with your skills and innate strengths means that you'll stick with the commitments over a long time.

Next Steps

What updates do you need to make to your MAPS so you continue in your quest to become a better ancestor? What methods (the doing), attitudes (the way of thinking), partnerships (the being), and skills and strengths (the having) can you make room for to help you align with justice? The Guided Self-Reflective Activities can help you navigate through these questions.

One thing to note—some patrons and workshop attendees state that they are not sure what commitments to make at this point in the quest. If this is true for you, honor where you are right now. You can reflect on the Guided Self-Reflective Activities and come back to it another time. Or you can jot something down now, then review a few days later. Another option is to focus on just one area of the MAPS so that you're not overwhelmed. Do what feels right for you at this moment.

I also want to add that you will wear out quickly if you don't weave self-care into your MAPS. I was going to add an extra S to the MAPS acronym but decided not to for the very reason that self-care, personal sustainability, and purposeful play must be woven into *all* that you do. It's not just a commitment thing—it's a lifestyle thing. The Active Rest Stops that were built into the Inner Field Trip quest were done to get you into the practice of adding play to the work. To be reminded why we need to rest and prioritize self-care, review Day 11. Ultimately, it is better to commit to one or two things in your MAPS and sprinkle in some self-care than to do all the things and burn out. Be discerning as you plan your commitments.

Guided Self-Reflective Activities

Step 1—Identify your mood before starting. Go to page 239 and use the Mood Tracker to capture how you're feeling.

Step 2—MAPS Commitments (15 minutes).

Supplies needed: Colored markers or pens, timer.
What to do:
✂ Set your timer to count down from 15 minutes.
✂ Using the diagram on the next page, identify the MAPS you're committing to that relate to the ancestor you want to become (review Day 2 to remember the ancestor you identified).
✂ Identify as many commitments as you can until the timer expires.

**Use the diagram below to calibrate your MAPS
with at least one commitment.**

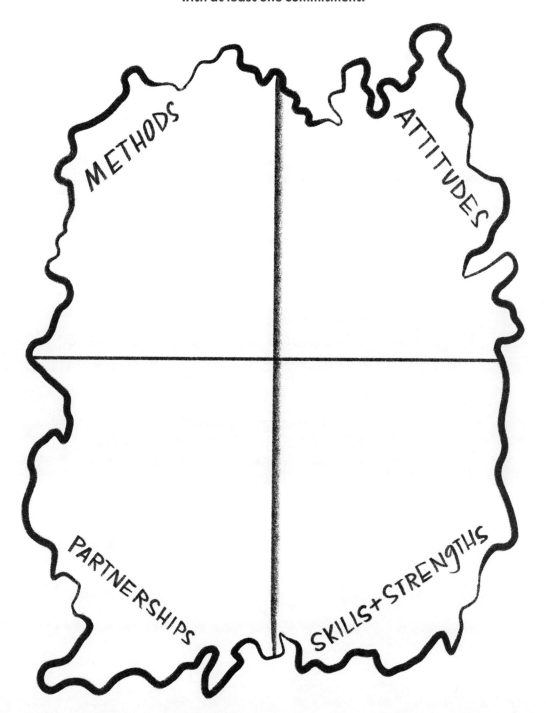

Step 3—Journal (15 minutes).

Supplies needed: Journal, pen/pencil OR keyboard and screen, timer.

What to do:

✂ Navigate the prompt using GPS (see page 237).

✂ Set your timer to count down from 15 minutes.

✂ Capture the ramblings of your Inner Oppressor in your journal or sketchbook using the following prompts as a guide:

Prompt #1: How can remembering what type of ancestor you want to become help you be more committed to the actions you identified in the MAPS?

Prompt #2: What patterns or behaviors of the dominant culture has your Inner Oppressor revealed no longer work for you? Which patterns or behaviors are you willing to courageously let go of?

Prompt #3: Which of your MAPS are you looking forward to the most? Why? In what ways can you celebrate your commitments without taking the focus off those who face identity-based oppression?

Step 4—Track your mood after completing the Guided Self-Reflective Activities. Go to page 239 and use the Mood Tracker to capture how you're feeling now that you're done.

Congratulations!

You have completed today's actions. Please resist the urge to move quickly to the next day's actions. If you have capacity, you can also file your Summary Report at https://summary.innerfieldtrip.com (optional). Otherwise, go to page 243 and color in the day that you completed on the Journey Tracker page, put the Inner Field Trip aside, get on with your day, then resume tomorrow at the time you booked to meet with your Inner Oppressor.

Your Internal Trail Crew

Up until now, you've been interacting exclusively with your Inner Oppressor. However, there is a part of you that has been patiently watching you and your Inner Oppressor wrestle over symbols, colors, doodles, and words. This is a part of you that had been repressed because you were so busy trying to align with the role that the dominant culture has forced you to play. As you cleared the dominant culture clutter from your body, mind, and soul, another voice has been coming in stronger.

Even though this book has provided you with the tools to explore your unconscious biases, the answers have been coming through as you completed each day of the quest. While I'd love to take credit for helping you get clear on the truth of who you were born to be, I'm not the one who should be praised. Those accolades should be directed to your Inner Tour Guide.

Your Inner Tour Guide is that part of you that is the keeper of the ancestral knowledge (humans and nature) that has been passed down to you from one generation to the next.* Your Inner Tour Guide is a voice of reason and remembrance. In other words, it reminds you of your values and beliefs that are not tangled up with the changing whims of the dominant culture. Your Inner Tour Guide helps you recall who you are beyond the false narrative tied up with your social, ethnic, biological, and behavioral identities (SEBBIs). It reminds you to release the guilt and shame around what you did not know or what you failed to do. Treating yourself with grace, ease, and tenderness is what your

---

* Carl Jung calls this the "collective unconscious."

Inner Tour Guide desires for you. Ultimately, your Inner Tour Guide is a repre-sentative of Divine Wisdom (also known as Trusted Source, Higher Self, intu-ition, God, HaShem, All-Wise, YHWH, Allah, Universe, or Spirit) and is fluent in the language of somatic sensations. If the sensation occurs in your body while you're engaging in activism, it's your Inner Tour Guide trying to get your attention.

Your Inner Tour Guide helps your Inner Oppressor continue its protective role in a way that doesn't diminish the humanity of others. Before going on an Inner Field Trip, your Inner Oppressor used inequities as a ladder to obtain power and prestige.* Now that your Inner Tour Guide's voice is becoming clearer, your Inner Oppressor continues its protective role, but in a way that helps it seek collaboration, curiosity, creativity, and community as a way to stay safe. When your Inner Oppressor feels tempted to look outside of yourself for guidance, your Inner Tour Guide reminds you that you have all the wisdom you need within you. Your Inner Tour Guide reminds you and your Inner Oppressor that though the Inner Field Trip may have rugged internal trails and dark inner caves, you are safe as long as all parts work together. Your Inner Self, Inner Oppressor, and Inner Tour Guide make up your Internal Trail Crew.**

You're the captain of this merry band of internal hikers. You still get to make decisions about what you will and will not do. In other words, you have a choice. You always do. Systems of oppression will still (sadly) exist after you complete the Inner Field Trip. You have to decide how you'll operate within these systems even though you now have a new mindset. As the captain of this Internal Trail Crew, you make the final call. Your Inner Self, Inner Oppressor, and Inner Tour Guide will not abandon you if you need to navigate public and private spaces differently than your Internal Trail Crew would advise. Don't be surprised, however, if your Internal Trail Crew files a grievance report to you, the captain, for violating your most important values and beliefs. In other words, your Internal Trail Crew will work together to reveal yet another uncon-scious bias you need to work on.

---

* Petyr "Littlefinger" Baelish, a character from the television series *Game of Thrones* played by Aidan Gillen, once said that chaos is a ladder. He creates disinformation and uses the confusion to make gains for himself. Littlefinger is similar to your Inner Oppressor (IO), but instead of chaos, your IO uses inequities to obtain power, prestige, and position.

** The idea of subpersonalities, or parts within us, is a concept understood within a few counseling methodologies. The Internal Trail Crew is influenced by the work of Dr. Richard Schwartz's Internal Family Systems.

At first, your Internal Trail Crew will have some tense, awkward moments as you learn to work with them and they learn to work with each other. For far too long, your Inner Oppressor has taken the lead, diminishing the other parts of you to survive within a system that exploits and dehumanizes. Kataleya, a patron, shares how her Inner Oppressor had a tough time taking a step back to allow her Inner Tour Guide (ITG) to help her find meaning.

One of my values is what I called "immersion," in terms of time, attention, and focus on people, ideas, and stories that are meaningful. My ITG helps me find it, while my IO tries to push me out of it. She likes me numb. So that's what I'm hoping to carry into justice work. Notice that IO voice when she's trying to get me to rush, to prove, to show "them" [gestures vaguely] that we're a good person & keep it moving. Instead, to take a beat & listen to what I'm drawn to, called to, by my ITG. Sometimes that might be engaging someone in a [one-on-one] conversation instead of reposting another person's story on Instagram and assuming they get the message. Sometimes it might be undergoing deeper research instead of doing the reflexive thing that is more transactional, like building a relationship to a group or community (like this one) instead of (or in addition to) donating to a national organization and calling it a day. All that stuff takes more time and intention, and I understand now why resilience is critical to living our values.

Another patron, Janice, also identified that her Internal Trail Crew was at odds with each other when a truth was revealed during the Inner Field Trip:

Something my IO and ITG don't agree on is that my IO wants to be less vulnerable in relationships. Perhaps it even feels like others couldn't give me what I need. In that way, it makes it hard for me to create or be in a community. My ITG knows that it's a fear of connection. This is one of my challenges, and with my Inner Mediators, I can continue making small and big decisions on my journey to unlearn old patterns.

Because you have been urgently trying to be perfect and diminish your accomplishments and achievements, it has been easy for the dominant culture to treat you as a marionette, pulling your strings so that you stay quiet and compliant in the face of systemic oppression. Your Inner Oppressor has bullied, pressured, and manipulated you into submitting to the dominant culture so that you achieve power, prestige, and profits. Your Inner Self has virtually been nonexistent as it has learned to hide and play a role that pleases external demands and aligns with the protective nature of your Inner Oppressor. You may think that getting rid of your Inner Oppressor is the goal of the Inner Field Trip. It is not. You cannot beat, overcome, or fight it. Giving your Inner Oppressor a new role or calling it by a different name will not work. As long as systems of oppression exist, so will your Inner Oppressor.

This may sound discouraging, but the work you've done over the previous 27 days is not for naught. Your Inner Oppressor is now part of a team:

- Your Inner Self reminds the crew of who you are beyond SEBBIs. You are your beliefs, values, lived experiences, and motivations independent of the dominant culture.

- Your Inner Tour Guide provides the crew with ancestral wisdom, the collection of narratives, experiences, and languages of the humans who came before you. It reminds you that you're influenced by the intergenerational wounds that have not healed, the problematic ancestors who did not do good things, and the good things they have passed on in the form of memories, dreams, and stories. You'll learn from your Inner Tour Guide how your ancestors solved systemic problems in the past (and how they upheld them). This is the wisdom you need to dismantle systems of oppression now.

- Your Inner Oppressor will still operate as your protector; however, it is no longer your sole inner voice, and does not seek to protect you at the expense of others. You may wish to also think of your Inner Oppressor your Inner Protector, but be sure that your Internal Trail Crew does not hesitate to point out to the rest of the team when the impulse to protect yourself may take the shape of numbing out to the dominant culture and trying to "fit in" at the expense of others—as well as at the expense of yourself and all your hard work. You can reframe the Inner Oppressor, but it cannot be banished. You need to remain aware, alert, and exercise patience as you slowly welcome it back onto the team.

Your Internal Trail Crew now needs to learn to speak as equals. None is more dominant than the other. The Inner Oppressor isn't the angry part of you, and the Inner Self and Inner Tour Guide aren't the more compassionate parts of you. All can show intense emotions depending on the situation. Yes, that means that your Inner Tour Guide and Inner Self can become furious, too. Your Inner Oppressor doesn't only tell you lies, and your Inner Tour Guide isn't just going to counter those lies with truths with your Inner Self as a passive observer. Be careful about envisioning your Internal Trail Crew through an either/or concept. Pierre, a patron, shared that the voices of his Internal Trail Crew are becoming more distinct as he continues meeting them on his inner-most trail:

> I found that my IO and my ITG have very distinct voices now. This gives me hope for a future with much less bias. I have a sense of strength when bias pops up now, I hear it in a different place in my mind. My IO's voice is smaller and from behind. My ITG is calm and from the right. It has made it easier to recognize the IO and thoughtfully choose next steps. Within the journaling, I was able to ask myself questions regarding how I move forward and can I say yes to them.

Like volunteers who help maintain a trail, your Internal Trail Crew will continue to journey with you on your innermost trail. As one of my Licensed Navigators shared, the Internal Trail Crew is "trekking the trails, keeping the trail markers clear, repairing broken bridges or stairs, checking the maps, and offering support to the thru-trekker—you." You may feel lonely while venturing on your Inner Field Trip, but you're never alone. Your Internal Trail Crew is with you at every step.

Meet and Name Your Inner Tour Guide

Like your Inner Oppressor, you need to bring your Inner Tour Guide to life visually. So, for this prompt, you will draw your Inner Tour Guide. When you do, please be mindful of harmful caricatures. Early in the days of the Inner Field Trip, I led a few groups in drawing their Inner Tour Guide. Unfortunately, what was drawn were stereotypes of Indigenous, Black, and brown people. The coddling Black woman, the magical Black man, the spiritual South Asian guru, the wise Indigenous elder were some of the images drawn by those who did not share their avatar's ethnicity or culture. I was alarmed that even after doing their work to explore their unconscious biases, some attendees resorted to caricatures of BIPOCs to imagine what their Inner Tour Guide looked like.

It's okay if you identify as Southeast Asian, for example, and you want your Inner Tour Guide to reflect your skin tone, cultural background, and ethnicity. If you'd like to make your Inner Tour Guide in the image of an animal or something else in nature, that's fine, too. Draw your Inner Tour Guide, taking extra care not to amplify stereotypes.

Your Inner Tour Guide also needs a name. Choose one that begins with an adjective, or a descriptive word, and then ends with a first name. An alliteration, where the adjective and the first name begin with the same letter, will make the name of your Inner Tour Guide more memorable. *Grounded Gertrude, Introspective Ingrid*, and *Welcoming Will* are just some of the names patrons have used to call their Inner Tour Guide. Having a name for your Inner Oppressor (which you did on Day 8) and your Inner Tour Guide is a way to assign uniqueness to members of your Inner Trail Crew.

If, as you're naming your Inner Tour Guide, you're finding that there's another voice that's coming through, it could be that your Inner Tour Guide is part of a council. Similar to the experience that some had when naming their Inner Oppressor, your Inner Tour Guide may be two or more identities representing different parts of that wise and knowledgeable part of your inner being. Don't treat the additional parts of your Inner Tour Guide as intruders if you're thinking that you have to stick to just one name. It is okay to give them all names.

One other thing to note—you won't give a name to your Inner Self, as that is the true, authentic version of you. Giving it a separate name, independent of your actual name, may create confusion. If anything, you can call your Inner Self by your first name with the words "true" or "authentic" or "real" or "sincere" in front of it. Using this example, my Inner Self would be named True Leesa or Authentic Leesa to separate it from the outer version of Leesa.

Guided Self-Reflective Activities

Step 1—Identify your mood before starting. Go to page 239 and use the Mood Tracker to capture how you're feeling.

Step 2—Name Your Internal Trail Crew (15 minutes).

Supplies needed: Colored markers or pens, stickers (optional), timer.

What to do:

- Set your timer to count down from 15 minutes, then draw your Inner Tour Guide.
- Give your Inner Tour Guide a name. The name you give your Inner Tour Guide should start with a descriptive adjective, followed by a first name. I suggest using an alliteration; in other words, whatever letter your descriptive adjective starts with (for example, an I for introspective or a G for grounded), choose a first name with that same letter (for example, Ingrid or Gertrude) to make the name even more memorable.

Use the space below to draw your Inner Tour Guide.

OPTIONAL: Give your Internal Trail Crew a name.

Supplies needed: Colored markers or pens, stickers (optional), timer.

What to do:

- Using the diagram on the next page, write the name of:

  Your Inner Oppressor (you did this on Day 8).

  Your Inner Self (that would be your first name with "True," "Authentic," or "Real" before it).

  Your Inner Tour Guide (you did this earlier in this prompt).

- Give your crew a name. Choose a name that holds significance to you.

  You can add "group," "society," "council," "team," "alliance," "club," "coalition," "federation," "circle," "order," "assembly," "guild," "cooperative," "league," "collective," "siblinghood," or "squad" to your crew's name.

  Some names, such as "gang," "caste," "mob," or "posse" hold harmful stereotypes, so be sure **not** to use them in the naming of your Internal Trail Crew.

  "Tribe" is problematic, as it was used to dehumanize the people that colonizers met during their invasions. Please **do not** use the word "tribe" in the naming of your Internal Trail Crew.

  "Clan," "band," "pack" (e.g., "wolf pack"), "syndicate," "house," "troop," "army," or "union" may hold cultural, class, or military significance to some groups, so avoid using those words in the naming of your Internal Trail Crew.

Name of Internal Trail Crew:

_____

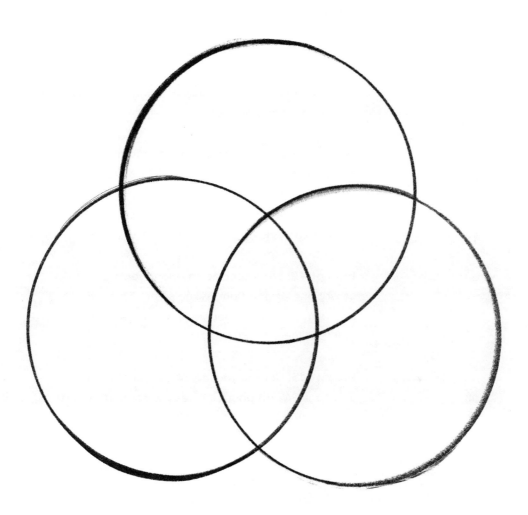

Step 3—Journal (15 minutes).

Supplies needed: Journal, pen/pencil OR keyboard and screen, timer.

What to do:

⨯ Navigate the prompt using GPS (see page 237).

⨯ Set your timer to count down from 15 minutes.

⨯ Capture the ramblings of your Inner Oppressor in your journal or sketchbook using the following prompts as a guide:

Prompt #1: How will you know the difference between your Inner Oppressor trying to keep you safe and secure, your Inner Self trying to remind you of your unique values, and your Inner Tour Guide trying to provide ancestral and divine wisdom?

Prompt #2: What specific emotions, feelings, sensations, or vibrations will help you distinguish between the voice of your Inner Oppressor, Inner Self, and Inner Tour Guide?

Prompt #3: How do you feel about your Internal Trail Crew? What about it gives you comfort? What about it frightens you? Where do you feel the sensations in your body, and what does it tell you?

Step 4—Track your mood after completing the Guided Self-Reflective Activities. Go to page 239 and use the Mood Tracker to capture how you're feeling now that you're done.

Congratulations!

You have completed today's actions. Please resist the urge to move quickly to the next day's actions. If you have capacity, you can also file your Summary Report at https://summary.innerfieldtrip.com (optional). Otherwise, go to page 243 and color in the day that you completed on the Journey Tracker page, put the Inner Field Trip aside, get on with your day, then resume tomorrow at the time you booked to meet with your Inner Oppressor.

Dump the Debris

There is one thing that I accumulate while hiking that I can't wait to get rid of once I get to the trailhead—trash. While on my hike, I put empty wrappers, used tissues, and other debris into a reusable bag so that I leave nothing but my footprints.* I carry this reusable bag filled with personal trash in my backpack, and the first thing I look for when I reach the trailhead is a garbage bin. I can't wait to unload all the trash in the receptacle so I can lighten my load.

There are things you've collected on the Inner Field Trip quest that you may want to keep or discard. Today, it's time to dump the debris—specifically, to toss out the pages of your journal. Getting into a regular practice of discarding your journal pages is a tradition that you can perform after completing each day or every round of the Inner Field Trip.

You may have felt a sensation in your body as you read the paragraph above. Questions may have come up: "Shouldn't I read what I wrote all those days ago? Won't reading the ramblings of my Inner Oppressor give me new insights?" In my experience leading people through the Inner Field Trip since 2015, the opposite happens. Instead of making new discoveries while reading their journal pages, they feel a deep sense of sadness, frustration, and anger. Some go through the pages with the equivalent of an editor's red pen and correct their grammar and spelling. One workshop attendee shared that they felt bad about the way they characterized a family member through their journal pages. Others detest the version of themselves that showed up on the pages. To avoid re-wounding yourself, I recommend not reviewing the words that you wrote. There's no need to toss out the self-reflective art since only you

---

* The quote, "Take nothing but pictures; leave nothing but footprints," is attributed to multiple sources and is used within the hiking community as a reminder to do nothing to disrupt nature.

can interpret it; however, it's time to dump the debris that is your journal pages.

As a historian, I recoil at the thought of getting rid of anything that someone has written. Written words can contribute to the future's understanding of how we live today. In addition, most of what we know about history has been written through the lens of those who were educated and wealthy. They were almost entirely men. So, getting the viewpoint of those who hold intersectional identities is important to our collective understanding of how a wider portion of society lived.

The difference between saving written words for future generations to read, evaluate, and interpret versus the words you wrote during the Inner Field Trip is that the latter often contains angry, whiny, and confusing words.* These are writings that you would not want anyone to find. Now, if you journal in a way that you would not mind other people reading your words or doesn't make you cringe, you may not have been doing the Inner Field Trip as it was intended. You should wince a bit about what your Inner Oppressor revealed because your journal pages contain its uncensored, unedited, and unfiltered rambles. Another reason you should get rid of your journal pages is to use the act as a sign of rebirth. You are only one day away from the end of your Inner Field Trip quest, and there's no better way to celebrate your homecoming than to engage in a contemplative act to help you grow. One way to process the transformation you're experiencing is to release the pages that contain old patterns, thoughts, and behaviors you are moving away from.

The process of dumping the pages is called "Anchoring." It's a way to set yourself firmly on a new foundation. There are three Anchoring options to choose from if you did your journaling on sheets of paper or in a notebook:

1. **Burn the pages using fire.** If you do choose to burn the journal pages, please do so in a safe way. One patron reported that she went to the rooftop of her apartment to burn her journal pages. As soon as she lit the match, the wind blew the pages off the roof and she was never able to find them, even after circling the building a few times. I recommend doing the burn on lower ground. Some patrons who have done this go near a body of water, put their

---

* These are the words that Julia Cameron, author of *The Artist's Way*, says are captured in your morning pages.

journal pages in a small pit that they dug on the beach, riverbank, or shoreline, light a match, then watch as the pages burn in the pit. One patron waited for a full moon, then burned their pages at night. If you do the burn inside your home, research ways to do it safely. You want to get rid of the pages and not inadvertently burn down your home!

2. **Wash the pages using water.** If you're not able to burn the pages safely, you can use water. Some patrons fill a bowl or sink with water, then dunk the pages in. They let the pages soak until the ink dissolves off the page or the paper turns into pulp. Once the pages are soft and mushy, the excess water is squeezed out, then they put the mound in the recycling bin. The act of "washing" the pages is like cleansing yourself of bad energy.

3. **Shred the pages using a shredder.** You can skip the fire and water options by cutting the journal pages into tiny pieces. I recommend using a shredding machine to make the task easier. If you have quite a number of pages to shred, find a company that can do it securely (you'll have to pay a fee). You may find satisfaction knowing that the bad energy and faulty socialization revealed by your Inner Oppressor in your journal pages have been sliced and cut away.

If you used a website, app, or word processing software to journal, then obviously you would not have pages to burn, wash, or shred. First, ensure that your digital journal pages are secure. If you were to pass on tomorrow, you wouldn't want anyone to easily access your words. Once you're confident that your digital words are secure, I recommend choosing an item that can stand in the gap of your journal pages. In other words, use an object that represents your journal pages, then cut, burn, or wash that item instead. One example is to use a cord or string that you can cut into a few pieces. The cutting of the string represents your separation from the dominant culture. If a cord or string does not feel as if it's the right object to represent this part of your journey, choose an object that does. You can choose the "stand in the gap" option if destroying your journal pages causes your Inner Archivist to scream in discomfort.

Although I'm recommending that you discard your journal pages using the burn, wash, or shred options, you may choose not to throw away every page.

Going back to my hiking experience, I don't toss out everything once I encounter a garbage bin. Yes, I'll get rid of the used tissues and empty wrappers; however I keep the reusable bag because I can take it with me on my next hiking trip. I also sift through its contents just to make sure I didn't mistakenly add something that I want to keep.

This is the same with your journal pages. You may decide that there are some pages worth keeping. Perhaps there was a quote or prompt that you wrote down and you want to make sure you don't forget. There may have been one specific day in your Inner Field Trip that was so pivotal and powerful for you that you see it as a turning point in your life, and you may want to preserve remnants of that one day. Taking a photo of your writings or scanning them are options as well if there are some pages you want to keep. Just be sure to secure the photos of your writings somewhere where no one can access them. Also, heed my warning—reading your journal pages indiscriminately can cause you to self-oppress. If there is something you know you specifically want to save, go straight to that section and preserve it in your chosen manner without casually rereading other sections along the way. The burn, wash, or shred options are the options I highly recommend.

As you go through the process of dumping the debris, you may feel compelled to discard and donate other items you used during the Inner Field Trip. Cleaning your cozy grotto, the spot where you met your Inner Oppressor, may also prompt you to put the sheets in the wash, organize the space, disinfect the surfaces, and donate items that are in good condition but that you no longer need. After updating your MAPS (you did this on Day 27) and getting rid of your journal pages, decluttering your physical space corresponds with the clarity you're feeling in your mind, body, and soul.

You may become emotional today. Anger may build as you watch the pages burn. The tears may fall as you wash the journal pages. You may become numb listening to the shredder chop up the pages. Honor those emotions. Cry all the tears. Scream all the screams. Sing a sad song. Dance like Carlton Banks or Elaine Benes* to your favorite playlist and just let it go. Anchoring involves not just how you'll get rid of the pages but also the

---

* Carlton Banks is a character played by Alfonso Ribeiro on the American television sitcom *The Fresh Prince of Bel-Air* (1990–1996). Elaine Benes is a character played by Julia Louis-Dreyfus on the American television sitcom *Seinfeld* (1989–1998). If you'd like to dance like them, enter the character's name plus the word "dance" in any search engine to find videos of their iconic dances.

atmosphere you'll create to commemorate the journey from where you were to where you're going. Discarding your journal pages while it rains, during a full moon, or at sunrise can hold significance. Some patrons wait until the solstice or equinox to get rid of their pages. Photos and videos are shared in the Inner Field Trip Basecamp (IFTB) of those who do their Anchoring with candles or incense burning or the diffuser blowing. The process can become a second birthday as you celebrate your transformation.*

And let me remind you of this—while you commemorate the day you started your journey in becoming a better ancestor, you need to remember that Historically Undesired Groups (HUGs) are still being harassed, abused, surveilled, excluded, and killed due to identity-based oppression. Your focus must always include those who are marginalized due to their social, ethnic, biological, and behavioral identities (SEBBIs). If you yourself are a HUG, you may want to celebrate that you have enough freedom to have spent this time focusing on your Inner Field Trip, while many others who share your SEBBIs do not. Find a specific way of honoring them, not out of survivor's guilt but solidarity. Whether you are a member of an Historically Desired Groups (HDGs) or a HUG (or both), the end of your journey should invariably include remembering and centering the millions of people doing the hard work of shielding themselves from oppression, inequities, and violence every day. Yes, celebrate *you*! Be happy about what you've accomplished during the Inner Field Trip. And continue to be mindful of what becoming a better ancestor is truly about.

Guided Self-Reflective Activities

Step 1—Identify your mood before starting. Go to page 239 and use the Mood Tracker to capture how you're feeling.

Step 2—Schedule your Anchoring session. Use the form on the following page to decide what atmosphere you'll create to dump the debris.

---

* I call this your "braversary," the date you started your journey in becoming a better ancestor. It can become an annual event.

METHOD:	☐ Burn	☐ Wash	☐ Shred
	☐ Sift	☐ Scan	☐ Secure
TIME OF DAY:	☐ Morning	☐ Afternoon	☐ Evening
MATERIALS NEEDED:	*Candles, diffuser, photos, comfy blanket, crystals, tea, or prayer book are just some of the items you can include in your Anchoring session.*		
CONDITIONS/ PLACE:	☐ Bathroom	☐ By a body of water	☐ Office
	☐ Full Moon	☐ Solstice	☐ Equinox
	☐ Garage	☐ Balcony	☐ Backyard
	☐ Park	☐ Kitchen	☐ Diffuser
	☐ Sunny day	☐ Cloudy day	☐ Near childhood home
	☐ Sunset	☐ Sunrise	☐ Other

Step 3—Journal (15 minutes).

Supplies needed: Journal, pen/pencil OR keyboard and screen, timer.

What to do:

- Navigate the prompt using GPS (see page 237).
- Set your timer to count down from 15 minutes.
- Capture the ramblings of your Inner Oppressor in your journal or sketchbook using the following prompts as a guide:

Prompt #1: What are you proud of doing during the Inner Field Trip? What ways can you celebrate the journey you've taken so far?

Prompt #2: How did the weather, materials, time of day, and place contribute to your rebirth? Recall the emotions and bodily sensations as you commune with your Internal Trail Crew during this journaling session.

Step 4—Track your mood after completing the Guided Self-Reflective Activities. Go to page 239 and use the Mood Tracker to capture how you're feeling now that you're done.

Congratulations!

You have completed today's actions. Please resist the urge to move quickly to the next day's actions. If you have capacity, you can also file your Summary Report at https://summary.innerfieldtrip.com (optional). Otherwise, go to page 243 and color in the day that you completed on the Journey Tracker page, put the Inner Field Trip aside, get on with your day, then resume tomorrow at the time you booked to meet with your Inner Oppressor.

The Return to the Trailhead

*I*f I can ever use *Star Trek* as a life lesson, I will, and this is one of those moments. During an episode of *Star Trek: Discovery*, the ship called *Discovery* is catapulted 900 years into the future. Michael Burnham, who is the captain of *Discovery*, faces a future that is very different from the past that she left behind. She is stunned that the United Federation of Planets, the version of the United Nations in the Star Trek universe, has been reduced to one man—Aditya Sahil.

Sahil has been overseeing the only Federation relay stations for decades. By himself. All alone. The purpose of a relay station is to pass on messages. It's the equivalent of a server. If servers didn't exist, the many messages we share through our socials would not be exchanged. In the Star Trek universe, relay stations act as servers. Sahil does not know if any other relay stations are in operation and does not know how much of the Federation still exists. As a noncommissioned officer, he wakes up every day and does small tasks to keep the relay station operational. What keeps him motivated is upholding the principles of the Federation—liberty, equality, peace, justice, and progress.

After excitedly welcoming Burnham, the first commissioned officer to attend his relay station ever, Sahil asks her to raise the Federation flag. This is a task that only a commissioned officer can do. Burnham, instead, makes Sahil a commissioned officer so that he can raise the flag himself. While it unfurls, this exchange takes place:

Sahil: "Hope is a powerful thing."
Burnham: "Sometimes it's the only thing."

Sahil: "Our numbers are few. Our spirit is undiminished."
Burnham: "If there are others out there, we'll find them. We will."*

Hope can be infectious. When all else fails, hope can be the only thing that will keep you going. Hope without action, however, leads to inaction, hope-lessness, and despair. What you've done over the previous 29 days is action. Quiet action. The type of action that so many dismiss, despise, and diminish, yet is one of the most critical things you can do so you stop replicating a DEAD culture** within movements that are trying to bring liberation to all.

The challenge that you'll face now is trying to operate within an old struc-ture with a renewed mind. The dominant culture did not vanish after returning from your quest. It is still hanging around like an unpleasant odor. This reality and the inner work that you've done as part of the Inner Field Trip quest should awaken a craving to be in community with others who can relate to the pro-verbial bumps and bruises you've experienced along the way.

You are more than welcome to join the Inner Field Trip Basecamp at basecamp.innerfieldtrip.com to connect with other Brave Trekkers. For read-ers who have completed the 30-day quest and need a refresher, we host shorter ones to help you maintain this new habit. There are also monthly classes led by our team of Licensed Navigators so you can continue to meet with your Internal Trail Crew. Meeting your inner team and being in commu-nion with other humans is one way to preserve your commitment to living life as a better ancestor.

No matter what type of ancestor you said you wanted to become on Day 2, thinking about the next steps is what ancestors do. What does the future look like when millions of people treat each other with gentleness, compassion, and empathy? What gift do we give our descendants when we pass on a cul-ture that values rest, kindness, and life-affirming boundaries? How much bet-ter would the future be if we treated the most vulnerable in our societies with care and warmth? How much better would people heal if we simply believed them? What beauty would the environment reveal to us if we were in harmony with the rhythms of nature? How much better would our relationship be to the

* *Star Trek: Discovery.* 2020. Season 3, Episode 1, "That Hope Is You, Part 1." Directed by Olatunde Osunsanmi. Aired October 15, 2020, on Crave. https://www.crave.ca/en/tv-shows/star-trek-discovery.

** A DEAD culture is one based on domination, abuse, exploitation, and dehumanization. This is one we need to move away from.

lands if we prioritized Indigenous wisdom? Ultimately, how much better would we be as humans if all were free from oppression?

These are questions I cannot answer alone, but with you, we can dream, imagine, wonder, and take small, sustainable actions. Remember—what you've done is generation-changing work. You are most likely the first in your bloodline to meet your Inner Oppressor and confront the issues your ancestors have passed on from one generation to the next. We don't do generational work to pass blame; we do it so we can heal wounds and pass on lessons. The courageousness that you have shown will mean that your descendants, whether you're related to them through DNA or not, will look back seven generations from now and know that positive change began with someone who took the risk and breached their attachment to the dominant culture to make a significant change. Your descendants may or may not know your specific name, but they will look back, thank you, the ancestor who cared so much about them and their future, and say, "Well done."

Let hope be the very thing you return to when you're feeling overwhelmed. Go through the Inner Field Trip once a season, or at least a couple of times per year, so you maintain what you've done. Join us in the Basecamp if you have the capacity and need the company of like-minded people. Let the ideals of the Federation—liberty, equality, peace, justice, and progress—be your North Star, the values that will guide you as you continue the quest to become a better ancestor. Surround yourself with those who are choosing liberation and hope over bondage and turmoil.

I believe in you! Let's continue to dream about and work towards a future without oppression, one Inner Field Trip at a time.

Guided Self-Reflective Activities

Step 1—Identify your mood before starting. Go to page 237 and use the Mood Tracker to capture how you're feeling.

Step 2—Courage 30 (15 minutes).

	**Supplies needed:** Colored markers or pens, stickers (optional), timer.
	What to do: ✂ Set your timer to count down from 15 minutes. ✂ Draw the number 30 in a bubble format, then fill the space within both numbers with anything that reminds you of hope, optimism, and anticipation. You can use bright colors, stickers, or doodles.

Use the space below to draw the number 30 in a bubble format and fill it in with colors and doodles that represent hope, optimism, and anticipation.

Step 3—Journal (15 minutes).

Supplies needed: Sketchbook or journal, pen/pencil OR keyboard and screen, timer.

What to do:

- Navigate the prompt using GPS (see page 237).
- Set your timer to count down from 15 minutes.
- Capture the ramblings of your Inner Oppressor in your journal or sketchbook using the following prompts as a guide:

Prompt #1: What version of yourself have you met over the previous 29 days of the quest? How can you use this awareness to show up more authentically in dismantling systems of oppression?

Prompt #2: Suppose you wake up tomorrow and systemic oppression has all but disappeared. How will you know that that is the case? What will feel different? What will you notice? What would you be doing instead?

Prompt #3: What do you still have to say "No" to so you can continue to explore your unconscious biases on a daily or weekly schedule? What support would you need to continue the inner work so you can work towards a future without bias?

Step 4—Track your mood after completing the Guided Self-Reflective Activities. Go to page 239 and use the Mood Tracker to capture how you're feeling now that you're done.

Congratulations!

You have completed today's actions and the entire quest. File your Summary Report at https://summary.innerfieldtrip.com (optional). Otherwise, go to page 243 and color in the day that you completed on the Journey Tracker page, then share your *Courage 30* on your socials with the hashtag #innerfieldtrip. Be sure to center Historically Undesired Groups when sharing what you learned after completing this journey.

Navigate the Guided Prompts Using GPS

Each prompt focuses on a theme, followed by three to five questions. The questions should not be answered as if you're filling in a survey. For example, if the group of questions looks like the following (this is Question #1 from the Battling Perfection prompt):

Question #1—Name a time when perfection failed you. What was the situation? How did you feel? In what ways did this moment liberate you from the yoke of perfection? In what ways did this event further bind you to perfection?

You would NOT write:

Name a time when perfection failed you.
At work.

What was the situation?
It was a rollout of a software project.

In what ways did this moment liberate you from the yoke of perfection?
I don't think it did.

In what ways did this event further bind you to perfection?
I quit my job.

This is NOT reflective journaling! Journaling requires freewriting and digging deep inside to more internal experiences, not just "stating the facts." Instead of treating these questions like part of a multiple-choice exam, navigate the reflective journaling prompt using GPS.

G = Go over and skim ALL the questions.

P = Ponder and name where in your body you're feeling what you're feeling (for example, if after reading a group of questions, your heart starts racing, those are the questions to work through).

S = Start the timer and begin writing in a stream-of-consciousness way, letting your Inner Oppressor ramble and take you where it needs to go.

Mood Tracker Ring

One way to monitor your progress through the Inner Field Trip is to track your mood. The Mood Tracker Ring is designed to track your mood before beginning the Guided Self-Reflective Activities and after you've completed them. Tracking your mood is a great way to see patterns and monitor your mental wellness. It also helps you become *feelings literate*. In other words, you start developing a wider vocabulary when referring to how you feel. This becomes important when engaging in social justice movements. Being precise (and not perfect) about your mood can facilitate better relationships and foster community care.

Here are some tips on the best way to use the Mood Tracker Ring.

First, take note of the related feelings. There are six emotions to track: *Happy, Sad, Unsure, Angry, Tired, Calm*. Related feelings are also included. Review the list of similar feelings so you'll know which mood best describes your state of mind and energy in the moment.

Second, assign a color to each emotion by coloring in the emoji. While marketers use color psychology to influence consumer behavior, you do not need to do the same. Some colors mean different things depending on your culture. So, choose colors that hold meaning to you. You can choose your favorite colors, bright colors, or not-so-bright colors. It's up to you.

Third, use the color in the Mood Tracker Ring to indicate the mood you're feeling BEFORE you start working through the Guided Self-Reflective Activities. For example, if you're working on Day 5 and you're feeling hopeless before starting, that feeling falls under *Unsure*. If you chose blue to represent *Unsure*, then you'd use a blue marker, pen, or crayon to color in the area above Day 5.

Fourth, AFTER completing the Guided Self-Reflective Activities, come back to this page and document your mood. For example, if you completed the activities on Day 5 and you're feeling drained, that feeling falls under *Tired*. If you chose green to represent *Tired*, then you'll use a green marker, pen, or crayon.

NOTE: Sometimes you'll feel the same before and after the Guided Self-Reflective Activities. Sometimes, your mood will change. Other times, you'll feel more than one mood before or after. Maybe the emotions in the Mood Tracker Ring may not perfectly correspond with your mood. You may be feeling tired, not because you're feeling worn out but due to fear. Feel free to cross out or add words as you see fit. Track what's true for you.

Finally, don't try to interpret or give meaning to your moods. You'll have a chance during the Active Rest Stops on Days 11, 15, 20, and 25, as well as on Day 26, to analyze your mood patterns. For now, simply witness your progress.

MOOD	RELATED FEELINGS
Happy	Amused, joyful, playful, curious, hopeful, delighted, excited, upbeat, thrilled, confident
Sad	Lonely, sad, vulnerable, empty, powerless, fragile, abandoned, hurting, mournful, gloomy
Unsure	Numb, disinterested, indifferent, hopeless, apathetic, aloof, doubtful, unconvinced, skeptical, blah
Angry	Bitter, resentful, frustrated, critical, grumpy, annoyed, displeased, fuming, offended
Tired	Exhausted, overwhelmed, drained, irritated, impatient, judgmental, bored, sleepy, worn out
Calm	Serene, composed, cool, undisturbed, peaceful, grounded, anchored, relaxed, patient

Journey Tracker

Color in the days you completed the Guided Self-Reflective Activities.

Tips for Book Clubs & Working in Groups

You may be eager to create a book club or small group to go through the Inner Field Trip with others. I encourage you to create reader-inspired book clubs, online groups, affinity groups, and in-person gatherings (what I'll collectively call working groups). Share photos of you and your working group using the hashtag #innerfieldtrip.

Given that Inner Field Trip® is a registered trademark, here are some guidelines to follow so you stay in right relationship with me.

Purpose of Your Working Group

The purpose of your working group is to bring people together, so you finish the 30-day quest together. It should not be to guide people through the Inner Field Trip® quest, nor teach them how to do the Guided Self-Reflective Activities that are in the book. Think of your role more as a host and not as an educator or teacher.

What to Name Your Working Group

You can use the Inner Field Trip® trademark in your working group's name for non-commercial purposes. It is best to use it with another set of words so that people do not get confused with the official Inner Field Trip® online community, website, podcast, workbook, and other branded materials. Inner Field Trip® Readers' Zone, Inner Field Trip® Fans, Inner Field Trip® Explorers, Inner Field Trip® Haven, Inner Field Trip® End-to-Enders, and Inner Field Trip® Hub are examples of acceptable names to call your working group.

Another option is to create a working group for those with a specific social, ethnic, biological, or behavioral identity (SEBBIs for short). Examples include:

Inner Field Trip® for Therapists, Inner Field Trip® for HR Professionals, Inner Field Trip® for BIPOC, Inner Field Trip® for White People, Inner Field Trip® for Intuitives, Inner Field Trip® for Students, Inner Field Trip® for CEOs, Inner Field Trip® en español, Inner Field Trip® en français, or Inner Field Trip® for Teachers

City-based working groups are yet another option, such as Inner Field Trip® Toronto, Inner Field Trip® Dallas, Inner Field Trip® London, or Inner Field Trip® Tokyo.

You can also use other names to refer to your working group that does not have the Inner Field Trip® trademark in its name. Calling your working group Guided Self-Reflective Network or Active Rest Stop Enthusiasts is acceptable. Let your imagination come up with a name that reflects the personality and character of the group you'd like to work with.

Words NOT to Use in the Naming of Your Working Group

Please do not use the following words in the naming of your working group as these are ones I use in my official community and can create confusion in the marketplace:

Inner Field Trip® (on its own), Navigators, Trekkers, Brave Trekkers, Basecamp, Camp 1, Camp 2, Camp 3, Stumblers, Brave Stumblers, Team, Online Community, Community, Online Group, Company, Patrons, Guides, Tour Guides, Internal Field Trip/Trek, Internal Field Trippers/Trekkers, Inner Field Trippers/Trekkers, Introspective Field Trip, Internalized Field Trip, Internal Trail Crew, Trail Crew, Inner Field Trek

Please check brandguide.innerfieldtrip.com for an up-to-date list of other words not to use.

What to ALWAYS Include When Creating Your Working Group

Whatever name you choose, please remember to:

- Include the registered trademark symbol ® in Inner Field Trip®.

- Offer access at no cost. People must be able to access the working group without paying a fee.

- Write the Inner Field Trip® name in English (your working group, however, can be conducted in any language).

- Provide a link from your working group to www.innerfieldtrip.com.

- Ensure that each member of your working group has purchased or plans to purchase a copy of the Inner Field Trip® book prior to joining.

- Add a sentence in the description of your working group stating that it is reader organized and not affiliated with or endorsed by Leesa Renée Hall or Inner Field Trip®. The exact wording you can use is "Inner Field Trip® is a registered trademark of Leesa Barnes / Leesa Renée Hall. This group is not affiliated with or endorsed by Inner Field Trip® or its representatives."

Visit brandguide.innerfieldtrip.com for more tips to avoid trademark infringement.

Commercial Uses of Inner Field Trip®

The Inner Field Trip® process is the intellectual property of the author. Charging admission to access your working group in order to teach the Inner Field Trip® process can only be done if you are a Licensed Navigator. To learn more on how you can become a Licensed Navigator so you can earn an income and use the Inner Field Trip® ethically in your marketing and sales materials, visit brandguide.innerfieldtrip.com.

Best Practices for Hosting
Your Working Group

I created guidelines to help you understand how to host your working group. Even if you consider yourself a skilled host, you may not know how to create spaces that are liberation-informed and culturally responsive. Go to brandguide.innerfieldtrip.com for guidelines.

If Hosting a Working Group
Sounds Like Too Much

Finally, if the idea of hosting your own working group sounds like a lot of work, and you really want to be in community with other Brave Trekkers, join the Inner Field Trip® Basecamp (IFTB). Licensed Navigators, who have been trained by me, lead classes and facilitate discussion in the IFTB. Thirty-day challenges are held quarterly and if you've completed the 30-day quest in the book, you'll gain access to shorter challenges inside the IFTB. I and other Licensed Navigators host classes each month where you can unearth your ancestry, create values-based boundaries, and meet your Internal Trail Crew. The IFTB is the only place where I hang out with readers, so if that's any incentive for you to join, visit basecamp.innerfieldtrip.com to learn more.

Acknowledgments

While the Inner Field Trip took shape in 2015, this journey started the moment I made my entry into the world. I first would like to thank the tireless and unconditional support of my mom, Lady J; my dad, Zek; and my siblings and niece, Marvelous, Seven, Princess, JR, and Mo. I can't write enough words to thank you for your continuous love, validation, laughter, and a soft place to land away from the harshness of the world.

To the team at Row House Publishing, thank you for seeing the vision for this book where so many others could not. Rebekah Borucki and Kristen McGuiness, I'm thankful for your excitement and encouragement. Gina Frangello, my editor, I'm thankful to you for providing feedback and virtual tissues when I felt I had no words left. V. Ruiz, Jillian Thalman, Sherian Brown, and the rest of the production team whose names I do not know—thank you for your care In bringing this book to life.

Part of my gratitude is directed toward my ancestors. Although they are long gone, I'm thankful to my African and European ancestors for the lessons they have taught me. Each time I add a new name to my family tree, a name that was once forgotten and now has been found, I reflect on the lives they lived. It Is through their actions, both good and bad, that I've been able to spot generational patterns so I can pass on healing and not pain.

I'm thankful to the lands I live on, which continue to sustain me. As a displaced treaty partner living on the traditional territory of the Haudenosaunee Confederacy, the Wendat, and the Mississaugas of the Credit First Nation and who has ancestors residing on the traditional territory of the Taino and Arawak of Yamayeka, and the Munsee Lenape and Canarsie traditional territories, I am deeply grateful for your wisdom and continued guidance on how to be in communion with the ecology and environment that surrounds me.

My dear friend Layla F. Saad has grown with me since we met in 2017. I'm thankful to you, sis, for your cheerleading, feedback, and encouragement. I'm also thankful to Andrea J. Lee, Paul Zelizer, Mike Gionta, Elizabeth Potts Weinstein, and Miriam Hall who each have influenced the Inner Field Trip® process in a significant way. To my cherished friends, I will give you a call and let you know that you are whom I'm referring to in this section.

Finally, to the tens of thousands of patrons, workshop attendees, and social media followers who engaged with the journaling prompts and made a spiritual, emotional, and financial contribution to the growth of Inner Field Trip®— thank you for having the courage to become better ancestors.

About the Author

LEESA RENÉE HALL is a mental health advocate, researcher, and founder of Inner Field Trip®, a community helping Highly Sensitive, Highly Perceptive, Deep Feeling, and Neurodivergent people explore unconscious biases so they protect their energy, align with justice, and become better ancestors. After a blog post she authored went viral, Leesa left an award-winning career in technology to focus on her passion—studying human behavior and personality development. As a counseling psychology graduate student studying to become a licensed therapist, Leesa uses evidence-based methods, such as play, music, expressive arts, and reflective journaling, to help her clients meet their Inner Oppressor so they decolonize and deconstruct while enhancing their self-awareness and self-compassion. Her advice has been featured in *The Guardian* and *American Express OPEN*, along with television, radio, and podcast appearances. You can find out more about Leesa and the Inner Field Trip® community by going to www.innerfieldtrip.com.